W9-AES-157

I DIDN'T COME HERE TO ARGUE

Also by Peg Bracken

THE I HATE TO COOK BOOK
THE I HATE TO HOUSEKEEP BOOK
I TRY TO BEHAVE MYSELF
APPENDIX TO THE I HATE TO COOK BOOK

*

I DIDN'T COME HERE TO ARGUE

*

Peg Bracken

HARCOURT, BRACE & WORLD, INC., NEW YORK

The lines from "An 'I' Can Never Be Great," by Stephen Spender, are copyright 1934 and renewed 1962 by Stephen Spender; reprinted from *Collected Poems 1928-1953,* by Stephen Spender, by permission of Random House, Inc. "The Brewer's Man" by L. A. G. Strong is from his book *Dublin Days,* and is reprinted by permission of A. D. Peters & Company. The lines by Stephen Vincent Benét are from his *A Child Is Born,* published by Holt, Rinehart & Winston, Inc., and are reprinted by permission of Brandt & Brandt.

First edition

Library of Congress Catalog Card Number: 72-78864

Printed in the United States of America

For Parker, with love

CONTENTS

PART FOUR

I Don't Know about You

AN EXPLANATION

IF THEY STAY WITH IT LONG ENOUGH, MOST people arrive at a point where their lives have rather a lived-in look. In some cases, as in my own, this situation awakens a long-latent house-cleaning urge, a desire to get things redded up. Sweep, air, throw out, put the rest of the things tidily in boxes, put the boxes tidily in drawers, put the drawers in a book.

Actually, this one began as a compilation of what I know, until it became clear that the book would be too skimpy. Accordingly, its scope has been broadened to include the things I have noticed, or suspected, or surmised.

It interests me—perplexes me, too—to see how long I have been noticing or suspecting the identically same things, with a consistency that indicates either a touching loyalty to first principles or considerable aspic in the brain cells.

But perhaps it points equally to something else that I've long suspected: that many people choose, early on, their own truths from the large smorgasbord available. And once they've chosen them, for good reason or no reason, they then proceed rather selectively, wisely gathering whatever will bolster them or at least carry out the color scheme.

Even so, with these truths of mine at the ready, writing this book hasn't been easy. Like many people, I have always had trouble knowing quite what I intend to say until I have said it.

I know a man (he smiles a lot and collects tin foil) who is writing the definitive history of everything, going way back to before there was anything. Clearly, this is a big job, requiring monumental research that he hasn't the money for. Therefore, he tells me, he is writing the condensed version first. Then, after it sells, he will be able to afford the time and research necessary for the book.

But my ambitions aren't so grand as my friend's are, and my problems aren't either, inasmuch as my ideas are condensed to begin with. Though this is a doubtful blessing, still it allows time for wandering down some back roads, which always seem more beguiling to me than the main highway, any day in the week.

There isn't much cooking in this book, though I've tried to explain my fragile affiliation with it in Chapter 1. Then, somehow, a cookie recipe landed in Chapter 3. Leave any door open, and cooking will plod in like the neighbors' dog. But I tried to keep as many doors closed as possible.

I'd like to say a word about the quotations. I discovered, early on, that most of the best things have already been said by somebody else—by people besides writers, of course, though I do think writers tend to say more good things than most, if only because they say more of them. This puts the law of averages on their side.

Indeed, there are some writers—Jessamyn West, Anton Chekhov, Peter De Vries, Loren Eiseley, Katharine Whitehorn, Thomas a Kempis, Richard a Bissell, and a great many others—whose work is so all-around satisfying that one would like to drop it *in toto* into one's own, providing merely a warm welcome and clean paper, if only that were allowed.

Still, even small quotations can be valuable, like raisins in the rice pudding, for adding iron as well as eye appeal. And so a number are included, for the most part in the Supplementary Reading that follows some of the chapters. I put them there when I could, because I have found, myself, that if they are scattered through the main body of the copy, my eye tends to dance from raisin to raisin, which is unfair to the pudding. My system also makes it easier, I think, for people who prefer to take their raisins straight.

Then I'd like to point out one more thing. It was Stella Gibbons, in her *Cold Comfort Farm,* who invented and perfected the technique of putting from one to three asterisks after her outstanding passages, to make sure they wouldn't be overlooked.

I wouldn't want to steal another writer's thunder, or her asterisks either; and her needs, for that matter, weren't mine. Anyway, since Miss Gibbons wrote that book, some advanced thinkers have refined the punctuation-mark picture. Now we have the Interrobang

‽

for sentences like, Can you beat it‽ And another—I don't know its official name, but I think of it as the Poorisk

*

which tells the reader there's a footnote down there but it's hardly worth looking up. And I, myself, have invented and perfected the Levitation Mark

O O

which indicates that the thing is still somewhat up in the air, or, This doesn't say exactly what I meant it to say, but it was the best I could do under the circumstances. For in spite of one's best efforts, the stuff will sometimes stick to the side of the pan.

In sum, this is a personal book. And it is personal in other ways. I confess to being the sort of person who's often asked a lot of questions. Like "Would you mind moving your car so I can get mine out?" Or "Isn't it about time you did something about your hair?"

But they seldom come up with ones that are any fun to answer.

So this book can, with equal precision, be called Answers to Questions I Never Got Asked. But I didn't come here to argue about them.

At least, I don't think I did.

—PEG BRACKEN

Please Be Seated Till Your Elephant Comes to a Full Stop.

—Sign in Disneyland

PART ONE

I Stand Foursquare, More or Less

CHAPTER ONE

My Feud with Food

"'Bring us a red California wine, a Cabernet Sauvignon, and be sure to chill it,' ordered Raymond Oliver, who had selected a seafood salad for his lunch. Then turning to me, the famous French epicure explained: 'I don't see why we should let our tastes be dictated by some code. I like red wine, even with fish, and prefer it chilled. Who is going to tell me what I must or must not drink with such and such a dish?' M. Oliver runs the famous three-star Michelin restaurant Le Grand Vefour, in Paris, and is the official ambassador of the cuisine Française."

—The San Francisco *Chronicle*

I WAS WAITING FOR A NEWSPAPER REPORTER in a large hotel lobby at four o'clock on a bright May afternoon in Chicago, or perhaps it was Detroit; big hotels are that hard to tell apart.

Waiting for some things can be unpleasant: for the water to boil, or for a taxi to show up, or for one's child to finish his stint in his piano recital, or for someone you love to telephone, or for the other shoe to drop.

But I didn't mind waiting for this girl. I could have waited with equanimity for considerably longer than I did, as a matter of fact. I don't much like being interviewed, and she was going to interview me as the author of *The I Hate to Cook Book.** (That is a book which rather eased me into the kitchen; and while it's cheerful there, now we have the new curtains, I occasionally like to get out.)

That noon I had made a speech to several hundred women, and I was beginning to feel unhappy about it, wishing—as usual—that the misery had ended when the speech did. With many writers it does, I understand. The marvelous feeling that it's out now, like a tooth left at the dentist's, makes up for everything, which is probably why they say Yes again the next time. (Writers are often asked to speak, these days, if they recently had a book published or if the group couldn't get the fashion show.)

But I find I'm about as uncomfortable afterward as before, with a tendency to twitch and walk on my hands or someone else's, wondering what I did or didn't say, or what I should have said, and feeling hot. Then the next day I generally suffer from spinners.[1]

But I hadn't started to twitch yet—was only standing there, under fair control, when the reporter appeared.

Her face was round, Irish, and pretty behind the granny glasses. She looked like a good cook, though she'd admitted over the phone to making my Stayabed Stew twice a week. She was a Special Features writer, she said, named Josephine Brisket (or Driscoll or Bixler; a fire engine went past just then).

* Harcourt, Brace & World, Inc., 1960. By the way, I have been asked by people who should know better if I had ever written anything before that, which is like asking one of the slide trombone players at the All-State High School Music Jamboree if he'd ever played the slide trombone before. Of course he had to practice holding his mouth right and working the slide. I've been a free-lance writer for most of my grown-up life, earning either my bread or the jam for it or both.

[1] Numbered notes are at the ends of chapters.

"Shall we go out to a terrace where we can sit down?" I suggested.

She laughed appreciatively. Sometimes people who have read my books expect me to say funny things, and they laugh heartily when I say anything at all. So I laugh, too, embarrassed because I didn't say anything funny. We can laugh it up like this for quite a while if we're not careful, and casual bystanders probably think some pretty humorous stuff is going on, though it seldom is.

So we went out to the terrace and took an out-of-the-way table under a large potted plant.

I have always found interviews difficult, from either side of the table. Years ago, I read somewhere that the one fact worth learning about someone else is why he gets up in the morning. So, when I was doing interviews for the college paper, that is what I asked the Dean of Women, who answered, with some asperity, "To go to the bathroom." Thus I learned that certain questions are too personal, while others, like "What do you think of our new lakefront development?," can be honestly answered only with an "I seldom do."

Too, as interviewee, I have few picturesque hobbies, proclivities, or even remarks to make, and presently the lead balloons seem to be rolling underfoot.

And, if it happens to be a good question, I can't answer it all that fast or truly. As a result, I seldom recognize myself in the eventual published interview because of these omissions, as well as some probable alien touches. " 'I'm glad Kansas City is air-conditioned,' chuckled Miss Bracken. . . ." I don't believe I ever chuckled anything, and if I were going to, I wouldn't chuckle that.

Josephine ordered a bourbon-and-soda, and so did I, and I waited for her to ask me if I really hate to cook.

This question always disconcerts me. But apparently there is a writer-reader credibility gap today. Write a book called *I Went Over Niagara Falls in a Barrel*, and they will ask you, "Did you ever go over Niagara Falls in a barrel?"

Still, in my book, I may have overstated my case to make my point; for I have, in truth, mixed feelings. And so, while we did some preliminary sparring (about the lakefront development, as I remember), I reflected that this might be a good time to sort them out.

For cooking certainly isn't all bad. Like television, it's the *dailiness*. And with some people, it is indeed one of the lively arts. And there are things that, while cooking, make the house smell better than anything except sunshine. (Hot Cinnamon Roll would outsell all the pine spray.)

Moreover, cooking is better than dusting the basement water pipes when it comes to getting appreciated. You never hear a husband or a little child cry, "Hooray! Mommie vacuumed the back hall today!"

Yet cooking has its negative side, and it is true that I have tended to accentuate it.

As I look back, my cooking career, to use the term loosely, was fouled up with writing from the start. The first thing I sold, besides some old clothes once so I could take tango lessons, was a household hint to a newspaper supplement for $2.00.

This was good pay for that particular suggestion—concerned, as I remember, with freezing leftover coffee in ice-cube trays to use in iced coffee. I don't know if I invented or stole it, though in either case it seems hardly worth the effort.

Then, shortly after the coffee-cube caper, I revitalized

Petunia, a character I had doodled for years—rather a cheerless cherub who looked like this—

I ponder with misgiving in
My rounds with broom and shovel
That it doesn't take much living in
A house to make a hovel.

(Perhaps I should confess here to a talent for innocuous rhyme. I saw a mediocre night-club act once—a man caught the words thrown at him by the audience, any old words, and hurled them back, woven into a long, lumpy, rhymed ballad. I think I could do that, though I would sooner scrub floors, or even cook.)

However, I presently transformed Petunia from thoughtful to troubled—troubled by rhymed domestic crises that I solved for her in a few lines of inflammatory prose. Then I found a cartoonist, Dan Bishop of St. Louis, who could make her do something besides plug along the sidewalk, and we sold her at the cost of considerable postage to a syndicate that printed six a week.

At first, newly wed and domestically innocent, I had a problem finding problems.

"What can go wrong domestically that I know how to fix?" I would ask myself, and the answering silence was deafening.

Then, in a singular moment of incandescence, I discovered that I must think backward: that the intelligent procedure was to find a fact, pretend it's the solution to something bothersome, and presto! What it solves was the problem.

(All unwittingly, by the way, I had stumbled upon an important technique in much commercial writing: the Reverse Think, or setting up straw men to knock over. Beginning writers might profit from my experience. If you know a lot about the P-TA, or fund raising, or sex tendencies in children from six to eight or eight to midnight, you think of a problem that your facts solve, explain, or ameliorate. Then you write your piece.)

And so I produced Petunias:

Fact: Small onions look and taste all right when combined with green beans.

Hence, the problem: Green beans are dull by themselves. (Actually, they're not, they're only beans; and like bathing caps, some things only get worse, the fussier you try to make them.)

Hence, however, the verse:

A fouler meal
I've never seen:
How large the bowl!
How dull the bean!

or,

These are the times
That try the soul.
How dull the bean!
How large the bowl!

or,

I never learned
In high school botany,
How to cure
The bean's monotony.

or,

I hurry in
To dine, and then
I think, Aw, shucks,
It's beans again!

And, hence, the solution:

Brighten those beans, Petunia, by adding tiny canned or frozen onions! Heat through, mix with cheese sauce if you like, and serve!

Note the swift, magical appearance of that cheese sauce, which would only take another twenty minutes. And note those exclamation points. No possible exclamation point was ever omitted.

Petunia was, in a word, neurotic, deeply troubled by trivia that wouldn't bother normal people; and in our thirteen years of enforced intimacy, which adds up to 4,056 little problems, I learned to dislike her with fervor.

Still, her influence went deep. So much verse of that particular kind can turn your prose into an idiot horse that won't stop trotting. Even now, on occasion, comes the sound of hoofs, the pitiless beat of the metric feet, pounding plain at the back of the brain. Once in a while, and some of the time, in spite of myself, the sentences rhyme; and I find it is usually harder to get rid of a rhyming word I don't want than to find one that I do.

ʘʘ Then there was some philosophical fallout, as How To became ever more deeply implanted in my psyche. Such is the power of habit and self-hypnosis, I felt that every problem must have a pat solution. Somewhere, surely, hidden behind the lost chord, there is a majestic Helpful Hint, comfort-all and cure-all for anything from the weariedest spirit to the stopped-up drain. (Though I haven't found it yet, I seem to keep looking—an attitude that has indelibly marked my approach to things, as I've noticed with some distress in working on this book.)

Most significant at the time, however, was Petunia's psychological effect. Roll around that long in dull green beans, flat meringues, heavy cakes, tough chops, burned cookies, lumpy custards, stuck drawers, cluttered closets, limp curtains, wilted roses, and tarnished silver, and when someone suggests you write a book about how you hate to cook or keep house, you don't just sit around swatting flies.

Still, it would be unfair to saddle Petunia with the whole thing. One's own temperament, I know, helps to shape one's culinary attitudes, too.

For example, a perfectionist will try a recipe called

Marvelous Meatballs. Finding them less than marvelous, she'll proceed undaunted to the next recipe, making meatball after meatball till they're stacked like the cannon balls in the old courthouse square, in search of the perfect Meatball, the ideal Meatball, Plato's Meatball.

But I daunt quickly in the kitchen. If mine don't turn out so well the first time around, I'm apt to reflect that I never liked meatballs much anyway. . . .

Then, looking farther back, there were the childhood traumas, and their dubious resolution. I remember my mother, whose mind was mainly on higher things, asking with gentle interest, when I was a little girl, "Did you find anything to eat for lunch?" If I came up with any sort of answer, like peanut butter, she would have some, too.

Accordingly, I felt that something was missing. A mother in a housecoat (Ma wore pants), unspattered by the hot corn fritters she had just deep-fat-fried to accompany the fresh fruit salad, *that's* what was missing. And so, when I finally had my own kitchen, I got some housecoats and some recipe books.

Which is when I started to hit the land mines.

Recipe titles like Sizzling Standouts, which were shoulder chops fried in tomato sauce, and Scrumptious Stackups, which were packaged biscuits cemented together with canned chili. And the economy dishes, the short ribs that took forty-five minutes and four ingredients that aren't ordinarily on hand. And the cookbook talk: "desired portion" for "the amount you want," and "piping hot" for "hot."

And I ran into some of those recipes that simply don't turn out the way they're supposed to, no matter what you do.[2] And the recipes that don't amount to much anyhow, like the Leftover Vegetable Soufflé that would have been all right if it hadn't been for the leftover vegetables—all the recipes that were passable but really not worth the trouble. I believe the one big fat cookbook that hasn't been published yet is a compilation called Recipes That Aren't Worth Making Twice. (I cheerfully release all rights to the idea.)

I must admit, too, that my own cooking reflexes were skittish. I was quick to correct the flavor with more vinegar when what it wanted was oil, or to de-escalate the muffins by opening the wrong oven door, or—in an out-of-character stab at cleaning up as I went along—to wash utensils so conscientiously that the custard was delicately flavored with detergent.

All this is hard on that poised, capable self-image known as the Altar Ego. It kept tumbling off the shrine. So, what with one thing and another, I saw Mother's point. There wasn't a thing the matter with peanut butter.

Then, finally, I was becoming tired of the word Homemaker, and the way we housewives were being eternally chucked under the chin. We were versatile experts—or so we were daily assured in the public prints—every one of us a skilled business manager, practical nurse, house cleaner, child psychologist, home decorator, chauffeur, laundress, cook, hostess, gay companion. . . .

On the contrary, as I wrote during that time in an article for *The Saturday Evening Post,* "We housewives are jugglers who, trying to keep a dozen nice big fresh eggs in the air, spend most of our time skidding in the shells. Once in a blue moon, for the fast wink of an eye, all the eggs stay up. The popovers pop, the checkbook balances, last month's tint is holding its own, and the children love each other. Providence hands out these moments, one or two per decade, as a tantalizing vision of what life could be like as lived in the center of the impossibly squared circle.

"But for the most part, we just mouse along, putting one

tennis shoe in front of the other, which is generally in the flypaper, bending over to pick up the floor mop and dropping the baby. . . ."

When I finally gathered, invented, stole, simplified, borrowed, and found a publisher for the clutch of reasonably foolproof recipes that went into *The I Hate to Cook Book,* I learned I had friends I hadn't known about—more proof that a mutual dislike can be quite as sound a basis for friendship as a mutual devotion.

None of us has any trouble rationalizing. We're not at all sure that conscientious cookery ranks up there with cleanliness in the hierarchy of virtues (if, indeed, cleanliness ranks all that high, for there's a limit to that, too). It is nearly always more expensive (*i.e.,* while a simple broiled hamburger costs you only the price of the meat, the salt, and the power, whatever else you do with the ground beef costs more ingredients and time). And it is almost certainly more fattening. If you've noticed, the most dedicated cook usually has the fattest or most fat-prone family—unless she is a lovely paid cook, that is, paid handsomely to cook handsome low-calorie dishes, in tiny precise amounts that allow of no leftovers.

One other point I'd like to make, because it bothers me increasingly, concerns the woeful things happening these days at so many festive boards.

The other night, we were invited out to dinner. The hostess wore a caftan, and she had soaked some oysters in cognac. Outside of that it was a nice enough evening, till we came to the *pièce de résistance,* which I couldn't help wishing our hostess had resisted harder.

It was an inscrutable turkey dish she'd first tasted (she explained) in a French restaurant in New York, then luckily found in a magazine on the flight home. She explained further that the recipe involved, among other things, marinating the cut-up breast meat in brandy, shallots, and various seasonings.

I thought it was no way to treat a turkey. I'd rather have had Mrs. Hunkerpacker's Stuffed Turkey, any day. (Mrs. Hunkerpacker cut a real swath with hers at the Presbyterian Church Organ Fund Gala in Clayton, Missouri, back in 1932.) I don't know what she stuffed it with, besides respect, but you should have seen the clean plates. I can't say the same for the French turkey dish, though I'm sure we all did our best.

As Henri Gault has asked, "Why this dictatorship of the French cuisine? I am especially curious since nine times out of ten, only a caricature of it is served."

Indeed, multitudinous mistakes are being made around our country, as well as over it—there's always that 33,000-feet *haute cuisine* in the flying machine—in the name of fancy French cooking. This is largely due to its minor temples that keep popping up like toadstools from Dinner Forks, New Jersey, clear to One Long Hoot, Wyoming, including Portland, Oregon, where they spell French even funnier than they cook it. No town seems immune, including San Francisco (a suburb of the village in which I live).

These places take down the sign that said "Mom Does the Cooking." Then, if they don't hang one up that says "Chuck's Chinese Pizza Château Featuring Mexican Wienerschnitzel"—as they well may—it will say, simply, "Chez Charles," in which case there is always a maître d' *en croûte*.

Then they turn off most of the lights in the dining room —probably because it is a dispiriting thing to see strong men weep—and they turn them all off in the kitchen, judging by what comes out of it.

But in many a restaurant I believe it's still Mom back there, manfully throwing another bottle of booze into the *bourguignonne*. And in others—I have this from an unimpeachable source—all in the dark of the moon, great frozen-storage trucks pull up and transfer their chilly innards—hundreds of neat boxes—to the restaurant's own frozen-storage compartments, right next to its infrared ovens. Which is why those restaurants can serve anything at the drop of a menu. A long, long menu. You can seldom trust a long, long menu. Nor an extra-cute menu, for that matter. Many a restaurant seems to employ more copy writers than cooks.

And so the lady at home, unduly influenced by these shenanigans, too often feels guilty about serving something plain. Hence the oysters in the cognac.

I know, from even my limited experience, that few things this side of the angel choir are lovelier than superb French cooking done—usually—by a superb French chef. He has come up from the root cellar, so to speak, and gone through the chairs as a good chef should, from soups to soufflés, giving prayerful attention to every nuance of taste and texture, as well as to the genealogy and condition of his every ingredient. He learned his food the way Mark Twain learned his river—upside down, wrong end first, inside out, fore-and-aft and thortships.

I know, too, that probably the best cooking of all—French and otherwise—is being done in this country by women in their own homes. Women like the meatball lady, women with flair, women who take it as a personal and creative challenge, who are doing their thing, marching to their own drumbeat; and they are welcome to it.

As for the rest of us, we go along more or less with Mrs. Hunkerpacker—less rather than more. For Mrs. H. spent a really ungodly amount of time on her cooking. Today we are able to achieve substantially the same effect she did with far less effort.

In the past decade alone, such magic has happened in the food field that Mrs. H. is undoubtedly whirling. (She left us for that Big Kitchen Up Yonder, one summer night in 1953, after eating too much strawberry shortcake.)

In fact, the war is over for those of us in this curiously affluent segment of our curious globe who hate to cook. Never could one cook so little and eat so well, thanks to the ready-mixed people and the frozen people. It is even a great day for the cooks who love to, for they can now give their single-minded attention to one superb dish, with the comfortable knowledge that the *croissants* are frozen and waiting, and the soup, too.

Of course, there are a few little problems left. Something we must fight is the dissemination of the idea that just because some things are easier to do, one should do more of them.

Then there remains the natural feminine desire to be different—not terribly different, but somewhat (for what everyone has or can get, not everyone wants, except for a few basics like fingers and toes and money and love). If Larks' Tongues Madère are beautifully prepared, cheap enough, and all over, the knowing hostess will do something unusual with hot dogs.

And then there's another small, purely practical problem for recipe writer and recipe reader alike, as I know from my own experience as both. Now that more and more good recipes start at the halfway point—"Add a package of This to a can of That"—it's often hard to figure out what they're talking about, for the reason that neither magazines nor books like to mention the name of the brand.*

And so one finds baffling circumlocutions. A recipe will call for

> One 11-oz. pckg. pudding cakemix containing alkali-processed cocoa, salt, mono, and diglycerides

meaning Doaks' Pudding Cakemix. But the befuddled reader, possibly with six boxes of Doaks on her shelf, will think, My goodness, I never heard of it, and pass right on.

Still, what minor matters these are! The experts will think of something. They've thought of everything else. And as for secrecy, who cares? Should the other ladies guess that you didn't make that nice creamy cheesecake from scratch (even though you did confuse the issue as best you could with chopped ginger), you'll simply have to do something else, like rise above it. For there are more things to do than cook, in this many-colored world, and miles to go before we sleep. . . .

Still, it all seemed a tall horse to curry, especially on such a pretty spring day.

So when Josephine leaned forward and said, "I'll bet everyone asks you this, but do you really hate to cook?" I thought awhile.

"Well, *part* of the time," I said, judiciously. "I think everyone hates to cook *part* of the time, don't you?"

Then I averted my eyes as she wrote down Chuckle, to watch a little girl at the next table fish the fruit out of her Shirley Temple, and I wondered how it would feel to have

* Magazines don't because Jones' Cakemix will be miffed if the recipe demands Doaks' Cakemix when both Jones and Doaks are advertisers. Books don't because editors know that readers are a suspicious lot (often with good reason) and may suspect that the author mentioned the name in exchange for a raft of cakemix.

a drink named after you—better than a disease or a hurricane, anyway—and I wondered if little kids will still be drinking Shirley Temples even after the Shirley Temple reruns stop, if they ever do. Then I thought of the Ginger Rogers Sandwich, No. 37 on the menu at Reuben's in New York—Nova Scotia salmon and cream cheese and crumbled French-fried onions on pumpernickel—and I wondered if I could find one in Detroit, or Minneapolis, or wherever it was I was.

NOTES

1. "A *spinner* is a memory of some word or deed performed by you which spins you right out of bed the next morning. It was invented, or discovered, by Kevin Keating, the general manager of the California Seals, who says: 'A spinner is always horizontal. Some are only quarter-spinners, some are half-spinners, and some I have had recently drill you right into the wall.' "

—ROBERT DE ROOS, The San Francisco *Chronicle*

2. ". . . The dessert at dinner that evening was Caramel Soufflé, a delectable light concoction that once took the fancy of Lady Bird Johnson when she lunched there. The hostess quickly supplied her with the recipe which, said pretty social secretary Sandy Bregman, calls for only two ingredients, eggs and sugar. But when it was tried at the White House it didn't bear any resemblance to the one cooked at the embassy. Both White House social secretary Bess Abell and Sandy then stood by the chef and watched him make the dessert again, yet when each tried out the recipe in her own kitchen, each experienced an embarrassing failure. To this date the presidential table has yet to be graced with the dessert that is cooked in a mold, looks like crème caramel, and tastes like a bit of heavenly cloud."

—BETTY BEAL, The Hall Syndicate

QUESTIONS & TOPICS FOR DISCUSSION

1. Are there more Gourmet Restaurants than there are gourmets?
   How come?

2. When you get a hotel continental breakfast that costs you $2.75 plus tip, what continent are you on?

3. What happens to steak that goes to Salisbury?

SUPPLEMENTARY READING

"Acute embarrassment seizes me when I appear in public not as my own mere self but as an art critic, celebrity of any kind, no matter how petty. Why? It must be in part at least because I feel something ungenuine, unreal, in being taken and appreciated for what seems to me so little connected with my kernel of self, my ownness, so to speak. It is an imposed pose, liked perhaps by individuals who feel inferior to the temporary role they are playing, like travelers who during a tour allow themselves a more expensive life than the one they have at home. And just as these strike me as vulgar, so does (I cannot help it) the individual enjoying praise, celebration, beyond his real self as a person. Anyway, I feel a contradiction that annoys and bothers me."

—BERNARD BERENSON

"Writing is dangerous, chance-taking. You've got to be willing to make a fool of yourself, to give yourself away. Speech making is the same only more so—and in public where you must continue even though the scorn for the spectacle you're making of yourself will be visible."

—JESSAMYN WEST

CHAPTER TWO

Report on Hamlet

"One thing I noticed right away when I came to live in the small town is they are always talking about something that used to be here but isn't any more."

—RICHARD BISSELL

THERE WAS A GOAT USED TO LIVE ON THE hillside as you came into the town, kind of a one-goat Welcome Committee. And when he finally died of a heart attack, somebody stuffed him and mounted him, only first they dyed him black and stretched his neck out another foot and put his horns on backward. Doggonedest-looking goat you ever saw. Hung in the pub for years. Don't know what ever happened to him.

There used to be an eating place on Main Street where everybody went, Sunday nights. Just family-style—you know, pot roast, fried chicken, like that. Big platters of corn on the cob, too, 75¢ for the whole dinner, and all the kids helped scrape dishes and wash up afterward. But that's long gone. . . .

There was a lady used to go up the hill every afternoon behind the post office and scream. Just stand there, you know, scream her head off. Don't know what ever happened to her. . . .

The town I live in—I'll call it Hamlet—is one of those places where the City Limits signs would be back to back if we had any, for the hard-core population numbers about 350, not counting the clams. It is a little northern California beach town with an inland lagoon—an arm of the sea that washes in and out with the tides, highly regarded by the blue herons and the pelicans and the painters and the naturalists. It has a nice backdrop, too, big lumbering hills soft as heaped sugar, fresh green in November and brown come June, in accord with curious California custom.

I said "beach town," though I would rather say seaside village. Beach town smacks of sand in the mayonnaise and a shooting gallery next to the taffy concession; and so far we have neither one.

Still, beach town probably gives a clearer picture: a scatter of houses by the bay, plus a garage and a grocery store and an antique shop and a pub and a post office and two real-estate offices and an overpriced spaghetti house and a six-unit motel.

That's all the motel we need, for we're rather hard to find as well as to get to, over a mountain via a corkscrew road or an equally perilous ocean path—only a diverticulum off the beaten highway. Just a pocketful of odd things, many of which aren't here any more.

Our handful of houses in the heart of the town is weather-beaten, salt-bitten, and for the most part old, with a faint New England accent. Hamlet happened before split-levels. Many a roof would shed tons of snow it will never see; it doesn't snow here. The mean temperature is about 60°, though it gets meaner fast when the hard winds blow from the water. Then the brass monkeys gallop for shelter.

But New England is losing ground. Now the town has a split feel, the girls with silver lipstick and dirty feet swinging their transistor radios down a main street like a shabby *High Noon* set. It all needs paint, and the gutters choke up with popsicle sticks, candy wrappers, cola cans. . . .

The village used to have a regular Clean-up Day, like a party. Once or twice a year, the men and the kids pitched in—raked, swept, shoveled, painted—while the women cooked.

We don't do that any more, though it could stand it. (An odd group recently moved into a little house farther down the main street and kept a horse in a front yard the size of an average living-room rug. Can you imagine? Wall-to-wall straw and manure.)

So the New England look is fast vanishing, as the architecture changes, too. California flattops are alive and swinging on the mesa, a high windy confusion of pocked muddy roads and raw redwood on stilts.

We have another mesa, too, by the way. It is called The Little Mesa. The main street runs between them, like a crick through a gulch. Once, there was a rugged, nearly vertical path climbing to it from the main street. It was a good walk before bedtime; knocked the kids out like they'd been poleaxed. But the path is gone now. A mud slide came along and, later, a blackberry thicket.

On quiet weekdays, the town has an air of waiting, awkwardly, to be discovered. But city slickers who discover it and ask around about prices usually go away talking to themselves. (Really, it's surprising you can sell beach property at all. That wild, wet chemistry of the water and sky keeps changing things—the waves forever lapping the jetty, lambasting the bulkheads, reshaping the shore line—and the cliffs keep crumbling, tumbling down. But the prices don't.)

Hamlet's people would have been easier to describe a couple of generations ago. That was a simpler time, when a summer place meant a summer place, when families packed the steamer trunks for a good three months' stretch and settled in. Then, there were two groups—the summer folk, and the townsfolk, who made their money here, one way or another.

Now the children and grandchildren of the steamer-trunk set have inherited the houses and use them mainly for occasional weekends. They phone ahead to check the weather. If it is pleasant, they come, aggressively denimed. If it is miserable, they go elsewhere. There are, after all, many places to go now. Like as not, their children take Hamlet on sufferance anyway.

As for the townsfolk, or year-rounders, we are a mixed bag. People live here for any number of reasons—a very few because they work here, the rest because they are lazy, or frightened, or despairing, or independent, or averse to interruptions, or because they were spun off the merry-go-round, or because they were born here and haven't figured out yet what to do about it; the same reasons, I suppose, that people live in a big-city apartment.

Or because they like a fine broad edge to things, or like the hills and sea and uncluttered sky, or the way the sun sets over the lagoon.

Or because they have a horse and want to live near it, not as near as the main-street people, but on one of the rolling ranches to the north of the town. Hamlet has one tennis court, too, generally unoccupied, with a sign that is gradually losing its letters. O BIKES, O KATES, it says, which has a nice lyric feel on a fresh morning.

In Hamlet, we haven't the classic small-town dramatis personae—no Town Rich Man, for instance. Or, anyway, we don't know for sure who he is. With no bank here, we've no spies in a position to report. Clothes are no clue, for people wear what they have handy; and as one Hamletonian put it ruefully, you don't hardly know whom to snoot.

We haven't a Town Bad Girl either, at least that I know of. Only some extra-hospitable ladies engaged in meaningful confrontations or valid relationships or whatever it is called now.

And while we have some crime, of course, it's mainly picayune. There's the way the candy bars and cupcakes melt out of the grocery store, days when the surf's up. Still, the kids have to eat, don't they? And the way the marijuana patches come and go like jonquils, or fever blisters.

And it is rumored that when a scared, sick, broke old lady finally had to put her lot up for sale, at a modest $3,000, a pillar of the community waved $2,500 cash under her nose and acquired it, then—shortly thereafter—sold half of it for $15,000. But business is business, isn't it? And anyway, it is only a rumor.

As for Village Idiot, there would be a dozen nominations if the matter ever came up, but it would take time to arrive at a majority vote. (We can't decide anything fast here.)

Anyway, we are kinder than that. We have Characters, not Idiots. Like the rugged old man who's wandered around for years, buttonholing people. "Hey, wait a minute! Here I am! About to die! And nobody knows about it!" The fresh enormity (or enormous freshness) of the fact seems to stay with him.

"But you're *not,*" I assured him once. "What do *you* know

about it?" he barked, and I could see that I'd said the wrong thing, and I was sorry.

And we employ other euphemisms. When the ex-Methodist minister pounds on the door at two in the morning, wanting to read aloud from his Lenny Bruce, we admit that he is a sweet guy with problems. When the old lady who makes canapés for the raccoons—just leaves them on her front stoop every night like cookies for Santa Claus, can you believe it?—comes rollicking down the pike in a hurry to catch a plane to make a screen test, we are understanding about it. "Hallucinating again," we murmur to each other, nodding gravely.

Certainly, the town has no social arbiter, unless it is the moon, with its pull on the tides and hence on the people, bringing them down to the beach to gather firewood, or walk the dog, or dig clams, or pop the kelp—for the air sacs explode nicely when stepped on—or look for sea anemones or sea stars or driftwood or exercise, or a new slant of light on the hills, or someone to talk to. One has many warm acquaintances here.

And the moon brings a few people out at night, too, down to the lagoon, still and silver, where there is probably a little boy trying for carp with a trout-size line, and a solemn egret, fragile against the quiet sky, his leg tucked underneath his wing. Poor fellow, he thinks you'll think, only has one leg. But just look away. . . .

Still, not too many people walk at dusk now. More and more you see the blue-white glow of television sets through windows. Reception is good here, a direct beam from the city across the water. And maybe they're watching a sunset in Rio de Janeiro on "Mission: Impossible," or over the Ponderosa Ranch, or something like that. After all, Hamlet's isn't the only sunset.

So there is no real arbiter, and no wonder; for Hamlet's

social diagram would resemble the chemical structure of a gaudy molecule. Connecting rods are strung with billiard balls, each one doing its own thing and probably thinking it is the only billiard ball doing anything at all.

It is a broad spectrum, from a former consul to a retired specialist on pollywog pumps. We've gentle retired folk, with money and without, and people who mainly travel, using the place as a *pied-à-terre,* and some charming troglodytes, molding or stitching or typing or painting or carving their own worlds . . . square, oval, or free form. And we have our Thousand-Island-dressing people and our naked-water-cress crowd, our followers of Zen and Gurdjieff and Mary Baker Eddy, of Arthur Ford and John Wesley, Warren G. Harding and Eldridge Cleaver, Goren on Bridge and Arnold Palmer and Julia Child and Albert Schweitzer and Yevtushenko and Dow Jones and Peanuts, all of us marching (or hallucinating) to a different drummer.

Too, the molecule has some free-floating electrons: surfers in their wetsuits, a constant in the seascape now, like a herd of shiny black seals, and the hippies.

The hippies started coming a few years ago, heading like lemmings for the sea, but stopped short of it, which in some cases seems a shame. Like dreary gypsies in broken-down caravans they still come, finding the countryside more than ever a haven, now so many of their city kin have become activists, a frighteningly energetic word.

In they burrow, usually on the high flat mesa, living on welfare, or what they can find or informally borrow, though some of them live on remittances—paid to stay away from home—and commanding, I imagine, a pretty good price.

Occasionally, a long-haired apostle of whatever-it-is will lope down the ocean road tootling a recorder, a delicate dawn-of-the-world sound against the waves. But for the most part they are sour-smelling and idle, vacant-eyed and high on drugs of one kind or another, making the reasonably straight world seem doubly fragrant, intelligent, and wholly worth bothering about.

Life is quiet here. Mainly we mind our own business, do whatever we do, get to bed early.

Of course, we go into the city, sometimes. We're not all that far away from it, though one must be prepared to sleep overnight in the car by the roadside should the ocean fog roll in.

But more often we don't, for the village virus can take over and bite deep. More often, in the evening, we huddle together against the dark, no man being an island. Then the fishing boats parked overnight on the bay see our lights pricking the black of the hills.

Inside the houses, houses variously furnished in Department Store Danish or Retired Overstuffed or San Francisco Reject or what the tide brought in, we talk. About the high price of pork chops, or who was doing what when the power went off, or the meaning of man's search for meaning, or the Aswan Dam, or the cost of real estate in British Honduras, or the Basque way of cooking tripe, or of painting, or what's trumps, or the current war (we tend to solve wars here more sweepingly and satisfyingly than the Pentagon does), depending on the particular billiard ball of the molecule. Or of children or grandchildren, or who came to town, or who left town. For people do leave, and, in extreme cases, even die.

And so the town changes, for no town is an island either, and definitely not Hamlet, with its lagoon to remind it of the fact. . . .

As it is doing now. For the churning atmosphere giveth and it taketh away, and, over the years, the lagoon has been silting up. Topsoil from the surrounding hills, softened and roiled and creamed by the fog and the rain, has been running down like cocoa, impacting to solid fudge on the bottom. The tides grow lackadaisical as the lagoon floor rises. The herons and egrets and sanderlings aren't around so much now, and probably the whole strange seething submarine nursery, the source of it all, feels that something is amiss.

And so it needs dredging, which 350 people can't afford to do. Anyway, we're all pretty busy doing our own thing, the way you're supposed to be now.

There's no telling what will happen. Probably nothing, for quite a while. After all, it took us two years to decide to build a Comfort Station behind the tennis court, and roughly another two to get it built.

Perhaps Hamlet will pass the responsibility over to the county. And maybe the county will sit on its hands. Counties have many problems besides small lagoons.

Or maybe it won't. Maybe it will dredge it for a sailboat harbor.

Or perhaps the real-estate developers will come to the rescue, for they see a splendid harbor here, with berths for 1,600 boats. With reasonable speed, they could improve the marine life right out of the water, under an oil slick loud with the chug of the outboards and the happy screams of the water skiers. We would need some big motels then, and a chicken-in-a-basket place, and more taverns, and a drive-in movie.

And later days may find us talking of the quiet old village to the children, and describing some of the other things that aren't here any more. But what does an egret *look* like? Look it up in the Nature Book, dear.

I knew a man who lived alone in a city on a little street he loved—loved mainly because of the small public playground across from him, which he found cheerful to watch. Then the playground was improved into a parking lot, which increased property values (as he learned when he sold his house because he didn't like living there any more). But he never found another place to buy with the crisp green money that he liked half so well.

> *"I'm very scared, Buster. Yes, at last. Because it could go on forever. Not knowing what's yours until you've thrown it away."*
>
> —Holly Golightly, in *Breakfast at Tiffany's*, by TRUMAN CAPOTE

CHAPTER THREE

*

The Sunrise Collector: What to Do till Your Horoscope Gets There

"Know ye not that a little leaven leaveneth the whole lump? Purge out therefore the old leaven, that ye may be a new lump."

—ST. PAUL, *Corinthians I 5:7*

SOME PEOPLE COLLECT PAPERWEIGHTS, OR pre-Columbian figures, or old masters, or young mistresses, or tombstone rubbings, or five-minute recipes, or any of a thousand other things including bruises, most of them satisfying, depending on the genes and the bank account and where the heart lies.

My own collection is sunrises; and I find that they have their advantages. Sunrises are usually handsome, they can't possibly be dusted, and they take only a little room, so long as it has a window to see them from. Moreover, I can't give way to the urge to show off my collection to my friends. I can only talk about it, and they needn't listen.

Where I live, the dawn seldom comes up like thunder out of San Francisco (our house looks across the bay to the city; it isn't one of those vulgar, breath-taking, terribly expensive views, but more of a genteel medium-priced view). Once in a while, to be sure, it's a wide-screen explosion in living color; and on some improbable mornings, the sun and the moon nearly meet, over the ninth wave. At such times, there is nothing for it but to drop the book (I usually have a book) and wake the family.

But usually, sunrise is a subtler thing, melting pinkly down the hills before it runs into the water. However it happens, I find it the right time for Rachel Carson's good question, "What if I had never seen this before?" And her other one, "What if I would never see it again?"

Then, some mornings there is no sunrise at all. Only a mountain of gray fuzz, like a long ton of the dust clusters often found under beds and christened dust kittens, probably by some homemaker in her manic phase. And sometimes the fog blankets the morning with a furry quiet, growing luminous only toward noon.

And sometimes both the sky and the ocean are wet pewter, with rain sloshing the windows, and something pounding with the hollow sound of doom, though I eventually learned that it was only the spillover from the stopped gutters, packed with leaves from the neighboring eucalyptus trees, which writhe in the wind, mornings like that, like a bad Greek chorus. (Eucalyptus trees tend to overdo everything —grow too tall, shed too much, smell too loud. Still, it is nice to step outdoors on a wet morning, under the overhang, and smell their essence of Vapo-Rub mixed with the salt air.)

Where I live is a good place to collect sunrises.

Still, looking back, I don't think place matters much.

Once, I lived in an apartment, where I saw the sunrise only by inference. When the corner bricks across the air shaft turned ruddy, and I was up, I knew the sun was, too. I remember spending some good early mornings there.

I've also enjoyed dawns in hotel rooms, out of the corner of one eye while I was flat on my stomach on the floor, which is the preferred position for plugging a cord into a baseboard outlet (they're never at knee level) to heat the water for instant coffee. Room Service has little to offer the sunrise collector, for it seldom starts before 7:00 A.M.

And at one time, I saw twenty-three consecutive sunrises in the Alps, all of such a blinding magnificence that they were hardly bearable, let alone encompassable, for outer space can sometimes dwarf the inner to a disheartening extent. More often than not, I would go back to bed, abashed and a little homesick for my old apartment.

It is the time of the day that's important, I do believe. For quite a while now, I've found the hours from four to seven helpful in getting work done when I was under the gun—there's always that.[1] But, more important, I've found them to be a hedge against personal chaos; against the feeling of being, if not lost, at least temporarily mislaid. And though I don't always need those hours, or use them, it is a rich feeling to know that they're there, and mine, if I care to pick them up.

The fact is, the still of the dark early morning is stiller than the still of the night. Not wholly still, certainly. The house ticks and tocks and breathes and creaks rather companionably, against the ocean's susurrus, and there's an occasional solid *thunk,* like a kicked football, when a wave slams the pilings.

But stiller in a different way. Maybe the molecules aren't up yet. And last night's voices have evaporated. Nor is the room murmurous of familiar things; it is too dark to see them; all you need is one lamp.

It is quiet enough then to hear a thought drop, or to get the news from another corner of the universe. This is the time, I think, to wander away from the familiar meadows and mine fields of the mind, into new country. But after sunrise, there are beds to make.

Getting up is, of course, the name of the game. And this isn't always easy, even when you want to.

It can help, then, to lie in bed for a minute, exercising your eyelids: squeeze them tight, then open them wide. Do this several times, and they will presently get the idea.

Then rise, with gentle dignity, assuming it's the right time. (When you are sleepy, it is easy to misread the clock. This has happened to me. You want to make sure that the big hand points to twelve and the little hand to four, not the other way around.)

Knowing coffee is ready can start you moving. A timer that starts the percolator can take care of that. So can a vacuum jug filled the night before—filled with something other than coffee if you like, hot chicken bouillon or hot tea, or hot canned oyster stew, which is especially heartening in winter if you're pregnant.

I'm in favor of something to eat as well as to drink. Preferably something good, like a piece of hot leftover pie, or grapefruit with honey on it. Or mocha ice cream on a warm summer dawn, or sesame cookies, any season. I think I'll put the sesame cookie recipe at the end of this chapter[2] so I'll know where it is; I tend to lose those three-by-five file cards. It is an excellent easy recipe that makes eight dozen cookies, the size of poker chips. If you want to make them the size of silver dollars, I can't help that, but they won't see you through quite so many sunrises.

Poundcake toasted under the broiler is also good, and so is Mrs. Manheim's homemade applesauce, though in order to get this, it helps to be a neighbor of the Manheims. And crackers and cheese are good—most gentle cheeses, like cream cheese or mild Swiss cheese, or Port Salut. Or anything else you think is good. I only mean, there's no point eating something like Rice Whoopsies unless you like them.

Raw eggs are a help, by the way, if you simply want to absorb some nonfattening protein and be done with it. I confess to a certain impatience with people who blench and gag at the idea of breaking a raw egg into a cup and swallowing it. It has a clean, faintly salty taste, nothing bad about it. These people have eaten much worse things, and so have I, some of them out of Escoffier.

You can drink orange juice right after swallowing the egg, if you like, and the acid in the juice will poach it for you, right there in the privacy of your own stomach. In a way you're cooking, of course, but you can't feel it.[3]

Cup in hand, then, and a wary eye on the blackness outside (sunrise or no sunrise, the black goes away, or at any rate it always has), you're ready to read something. Or read at something.

Or maybe you're not. Early mornings are individual occasions. Maybe there is something else you need to do. Push-ups, or jogging around the garage or the apartment, though I don't recommend it; it's still dark and you might trip on your bathrobe.

Or maybe you need to write down the dream you had, or a free-association account of what you did yesterday. Journals are good. To keep a journal is to have life twice, as Jessamyn West points out, though if you feel that once is enough, you certainly don't have to do that either.

No matter, *I'm* ready to read something now.

What I read seems to depend on a number of things: time, age, circumstance, and what I happen to light on.

For one thing, it's a good time to look into things you've no earthly reason for looking into. I remember, once, spending a tranquil hour with the U.S. Employment Service's official book of job opportunities available in these United States, which had been a doorstop in our dining room for years. Though things were rough at the time, still it was nice to realize that at least I wasn't a fish-ripper, or a shank-faker, or a jelly-pumper.

Or a cripple-cutter, or a felt-hat-body-starter.

Or a crusher man or a gut-truck dumper or a slip-up girl . . . For a while I felt like fortune's own cookie.

Indeed, things can register with fresh bright impact, before the sunrise. Take the affair of the street elbow. Somewhere, in some book, Rixford Knight was telling of his struggles to learn from his plumber why they call it a street elbow. He knew it was an elbow-shaped piece of pipe, one end male—that is, with the threads on the outside—and the other end female—that is, with the threads on the inside. But why *street* elbow?

And the plumber kept on explaining that it was an elbow-shaped piece of pipe, et cetera, and Knight kept on saying patiently, Yes, but why *street* elbow? Was there once a Mr. Street? Or was it used mainly in urban situations, rather than rural? And the plumber would say, Well, he'd been in the business thirty-five years, and a street elbow was always called a street elbow. And his father before him always called it a street elbow. . . .

A thing like this can add an extra dimension to the day.

But what to read then is large, vague territory. I believe I know more positively what not to read: the novel I was reading last night, or most things printed on shiny paper, or the morning news. Especially the morning news, because one generally needs an antidote before getting into it, like laying an olive-oil base before going to a wet party. Something, for example, like this splendid paragraph of Richard Carrington's, which I copied down once, to keep handy:

> If the earth's history could be compressed into a single year, the first eight months would be completely without life, the next two would see only the most primitive creatures, mammals wouldn't appear until the second week in December, and no Homo Sapiens until 11:45 on December 31. The entire period of man's written history would occupy the final 60 seconds before midnight.

It is good, in the early morning, to remember what rung we're on. Then, on the next page of my notebook, I had copied:

> Sure we hate. Sure there's hostility, open and buried everywhere. But that's not the whole story, and I doubt it's as much as half of it. That's the point. I think people love each other a little more than they hate each other, and that's why we can go on. In pairs and in families and in multitudes. Love has a slim hold on the human corporation, like fifty-one per cent, but it's enough.
>
> —PETER DE VRIES

I find those lines good to think of, even right here under the nuclear umbrella.

About this notebook, by the way. I suppose it would be called my own Commonplace Book, which is the name—should someone not be familiar with the term—for a book that is anything but commonplace.* On the contrary, it is unique, containing—as it does—bits and pieces that hit you personally, with the clang of planets colliding, but usually not everyone else.

* It's the same odd logic that gives us *invaluable* meaning *valuable* and *inflammable* meaning *flammable* and *unravel* meaning *ravel.*

This has been pretty well proven by well-intentioned people who have published their own treasured gleanings, which are moderately interesting but nearly always disappointing. Apparently, the words that have one person beating his head against the wall in sheer pleasure, overcome by a profound recognition or a fresh wind from a newly opened door, too often evoke only a So what? from someone else, all of us being as different as we are.

I began keeping my own Commonplace Book years ago, out of a canny Scotch awareness that it is a wasteful thing to forget as much as one reads, which is what I do, if unassisted. So I became more prudent. Now my book is fairly fat, and it is certainly the book I would take to the desert island. Everything in it has—for me—the curious power of perpetual illumination or amusement, from Richard Bissell's

> When it comes to constructing a good heavy paragraph with some A-1 sauce in it, I am left wondering who stole the tire pump.

to Robert Louis Stevenson's

> When the time comes that he should go, there need be few illusions left about himself. "Here lies one who meant well, tried a little, failed much": surely that may be his epitaph, of which he need not be ashamed. . . . Give him a march with his old bones; there, out of the glorious sun-colored earth, out of the day and the dust and the ecstasy—there goes another Faithful Failure!

But back to what to read before daybreak.

There is something else to consider: contrast. I mean contrast with what sort of a mess the rest of the day is likely to be.

I worked in a department store once, on the Flying Squad, a bunch of sorefooted dolls who slogged from bargain table to bargain table all day, selling overstocked flashlights that looked like fountain pens and fountain pens that looked like flashlights and quilted-rayon sofa pillows that looked like the devil.

At that time, with my head full of how many for $3.98, I seemed to require poetry in the morning . . . Hopkins, and Emily Dickinson, and Arthur Clough. And Stephen Spender:

> Central "I" is surrounded by "I eating",
> "I loving", "I angry", "I excreting",
> And the "great I" planted in him
> Has nothing to do with all these,
> It can never claim its true place
> Resting in the forehead, and secure in his gaze.
> "The great I" is an unfortunate intruder
> Quarreling with "I tiring" and "I sleeping"
> And all those other "I"s who long for
> "We dying".

I didn't really like the Flying Squad.

A bit later, living in a remote part of Ohio, with hardly anyone to talk to but the slugs in the vegetable patch, I found that Montaigne provided certain vitamins; and so did Dostoevski, who struck me as quite talented.

"As a general rule" (I copied this down at the time), "people, even the wicked, are much more naive than we suppose. And we ourselves are, too," he wrote, in *The Brothers Karamazov*. I was discovering, about then, that I was so naive as to be scarcely bearable, and his insight came as a comfort.

And again, "The man who lies to himself and listens to his own lie comes to such a pass that he cannot distinguish the truth within him, and so loses all respect for himself and for others. . . . The man who lies to himself can be more easily offended than anyone." That seemed to me one of those truths that kept on illuminating the landscape.

More recently, it has been Science with me—biology, anthropology, astronomy—when I find books that translate these disciplines into simple enough words. I suppose the reason for this is all the wild magic that is happening these days, making me a little self-conscious about the Ptolemaic world I live in. Well, pre-Ptolemaic, actually, with a scientific grasp that extends approximately to the hurled rock.

I know I'm not alone in this, though it may be that word-minded people are worse than most. The other day I heard of an incident that heartened me, when I was talking with a friend of the late C. G. Norris (author of numerous novels, and husband of Kathleen).

His beautiful new twin-engine Packard stopped and refused to move one day on a minor California road. A teen-age boy came pedaling along on his bike and said, "Won't go, huh?" and Mr. Norris allowed as how it wouldn't. At which the boy raised the bonnet, performed some small three-second operation, and said, "Now try 'er." Which Norris did, and the engine sang like a bird.

Norris sat for a moment in silence, then looked at the boy.

"Do you know what a split infinitive is?" he said.

"No," said the boy.

"Thank God," said Norris.

Still, there's no law against wondering about all these things, and in the early morning there is time to wonder a little, though maybe not later on.

For instance, this discovery that any one of your cells contains everything necessary to grow a carbon copy of yourself! If they find out how to do it, which they already can with carrots (and the way science bounces the Baltimore Colts off Telstar, I believe it can do anything), what would it be like?

Would it be pleasant to live in a town full of spittin' images? Certainly all these identical people would be *simpático,* wouldn't they? *They'd* understand that you didn't actually mean any harm that time when you . . . *They'd* know it wasn't your fault that time when you . . . Or would they know any such thing? And would they also be an awful bore? And would you be able to trust them for an instant?

Yes, and what if this new molecular biology enables us to generate a new form of subhuman species (another thing they talk about) that we'd use for our dirty work, like pushing the buttons on the electric dishwasher, I suppose. . . .

Well, I can tell you one thing that would happen. We would notice that a few of these specially bred zombies seemed to have more spark than others, and we'd get all excited and establish special schools to bring their IQ's up from 27 to 52, because we're always more eager to bring the substandard up to mediocre than to boost the geniuses. Maybe that's right. From the looks of things, maybe we've enough geniuses. But we've also enough mediocre . . .

Or consider a few words of John Pfeiffer's: "You are walking a biological tightrope between coma and convulsion, the possible results of relatively slight changes in blood sugar levels."

The scientists toss these things off so lightly. But that is strong talk. I'd never looked at it in quite that way. I know some days a person shouldn't have got up, but I'd never realized the extent of the risk.

Even so, now that I do, this particular morning, with the coffee perking satisfactorily, the contrast with my present snugness makes it rather a pleasure. Everything's all right so far. And there are some fishing boats parked overnight on the bay, looking small and cold, which makes me feel additionally comfortable. If science is going to try to redesign us, maybe it should see if it can do something about the tendency to feel the more comfortable for knowing someone else isn't. "God help the sailors," we say cheerily, and throw another log on the fire.

Then, I was cheered the other morning by Isaac Asimov's rebuttal to the ugly rumor that each of us is using only a fifth of his brain.

"The best we can really say is that one fifth of man's brain has an obvious function," ✱ he explained. The rest may well be busy, doing terribly important things; we just don't know what they are. So perhaps some of us flog ourselves unnecessarily when we're actually using every decent brain cell we own.

Now, it's apparently true that 100,000 brain cells die every day, and, unlike teeth, you don't get seconds. That's a large fact, all right, as well as quite a few small funerals. Perhaps (I thought) I'd better not postpone till tomorrow what I was going to do today, or I won't have the wherewithal to do it.

But then I did some figuring. Each of us has twelve billion brain cells to start with, and a billion is 1,000 million. So what, after all, is 100,000? I felt better. Why postpone till tomorrow what I can postpone indefinitely?

Twelve billion brain cells. (A teaspoonful of figures like this taken early in the morning clears the sinuses, I find, and settles the psyche.)

That is more brain cells than stars in the Milky Way

✱ *The New Intelligent Man's Guide to Science,* by Isaac Asimov, Basic Books, Inc., 1965.

outside my window, which contained a mere 100 million at the last census, which makes it a pretty cozy universe, compared with some I can think of. The closest star is only 4.2 light-years away from us, which is only a little over twenty-four trillion miles, and a trillion is only a million million.

So we're on real sugar-borrowing terms with that star compared with some they talk about, like 61 Cygni, which is a good sixty-four trillion miles away, or more like across the street and down the block, as galaxies go, and go they do, and so do we, wheeling clear to the windy rim of the expanding universe. Though I suppose an expanding universe has no rim. And no wind either, way out there . . .

These are exhilarating things, and so, too, is the moon adventure, the same moon I see over the water, blending science and poetry, bread and circuses, theology and twenty-four billion dollars (another resounding figure, that) in equal amounts. And with some of the wonder rubbed off already, so quickly do we become sophisticated. Still, before the dawn, a fact worn smooth seems to regain its quotient of the miraculous, to ring like a tapped crystal.

"The vast loneliness up here is awe-inspiring," said Lovell, in Apollo 8, as Borman focused the TV camera on the lunar surface drifting just below. They were lonesome already for our green oasis. "It makes you realize just what you have back there on earth. . . ." And, perhaps, more than ever, the importance of not blowing it up, as well as what a privilege it is to be aboard the twentieth century.

"And I was some of the mud that got to sit up and look around."

"And I was some of the mud that got to sit up and look around."

"Lucky me, lucky mud."

"Lucky me, lucky mud." Tears were streaming down Papa's cheeks.
"I, mud, sat up and saw what a nice job God had done."
"I, mud, sat up and saw what a nice job God had done."
"Nice going, God."
"Nice going, God!" Papa said it with all his heart.
"Nobody but You could have done it, God! I certainly couldn't have!"
"Nobody but You could have done it, God! I certainly couldn't have!"

—From the last rites of the Bokononist faith*

At any rate, it's a good time to be awake, or nearly so, and this morning's sunrise, by the way, was uncommonly fine, though at first I thought there wouldn't be any.

It was a surly ocean creaming under a black sky. Then, with great precision, the sun drilled a rosy hole through a cloud bank, and the water was sudden opal. A tremendous break-through, really, almost good enough to warrant waking the family. But not quite. Sunrise collecting is an essentially selfish and solitary pursuit.

Then something else happened: a hand grenade landed on the sun deck, though on closer examination it proved to be a large pine cone from a Shasta red fir, its carapace a marvel of intricately jointed plates. That is, I think it was from a Shasta red fir, though I've never been able to remember the names of things—trees, bushes, flowers, especially all the ones with the infectious-sounding names, the biennial psoriasis, the phlebitis that last in the dooryard bloomed. . . .

No matter. This pine cone was a world-beater. And perhaps—it occurred to me—perhaps the pine cone is the Missing Link. Perhaps early on in the evolutionary murk, a

* *Cat's Cradle,* by Kurt Vonnegut, Jr., Holt, Rinehart & Winston, 1963.

pine cone decided to live a little and evolved into an armadillo. If you ever noticed, there is quite a family resemblance.

But no, the armadillo is a mammal, which would be too ambitious a leap for the most ardent pine cone, I suppose.

Still, I must look into pine cones sometime. And armadillos.

Perhaps I will do that tomorrow.

NOTES

1. In Anthony Trollope's autobiography, he writes: " . . . It was my practice to be at my table every morning at 5:30 A.M.; and it was also my practice to allow myself no mercy. An old groom, whose business it was to call me, and to whom I paid 5 pounds a year extra for the duty, allowed himself no mercy. During all those years at Waltham Cross he was never once late with the coffee which it was his duty to bring me. I do not know that I ought not to feel that I owe more to him than to any one else for the success I have had. By beginning at that hour I could complete my literary work before I dressed for breakfast." I am still looking for an old groom who will work that cheap, but the principle holds.

2. GOOD SESAME COOKIES: Sift 2 cups flour with ½ teaspoon soda and ½ teaspoon salt. Now cream 2 sticks of butter or margarine (I use one each) with 1 cup sugar. Beat in 1 egg and 1½ teaspoons vanilla. Stir in the flour mixture gradually, then chill it. An hour in the freezer does fine. Now make little balls the size of big black cherries, shake them in a bag containing sesame seed, put them on a greased cookie sheet, and bake at 350° for about 15 minutes, till golden-brown.

3. Another excellent egg suggestion from George Fuermann of Houston: First shake the egg well, then punch a tiny hole in each end—an ice pick will do—and blow out the contents; then fill the shell carefully with bourbon. To serve, just break into cup. Delicious! You will notice that the eggy taste is entirely gone; and if you prefer addled to coddled, this might be just the thing.

QUESTIONS & TOPICS FOR DISCUSSION

1. Would morning be better if it came at some other part of the day?

2. If the author is so interested in Science, why doesn't she take a course in it?

3. "The U.N. General Assembly's main political committee approved unanimously last night a treaty to ban outer space as an area for nuclear war. The treaty outlaws the orbiting of nuclear weapons and the use of the moon and other celestial bodies for military bases."

—AP dispatch

How about that! Discuss.

4. Why do they call it a street elbow? Find out.

CHAPTER FOUR

*

It's a Funny Thing about Me, but Not Very

"You're not called on to like everything in this world. Nor to speak up about all you don't like."

—JESSAMYN WEST

"DO YOU WISH SOME COFFEE?" THE AIRLINE stewardess asked.

"No, thanks," I said sourly, wishing she'd learn English. Why didn't she say *want?* The Idiot Wish, like E. B. White's Idiot Please that you get from elevator operators: "Third floor, please."

"Me neither," said the lady seated beside me on the airplane. "It's a funny thing about me," she continued, "but I can't drink coffee after dinner. I like it all right, but it doesn't like me."

"H'mm," I said, mildly interested, for I can drink coffee

all night and it doesn't bother me a bit. But on the other hand . . .

"It's a funny thing about me," I said, "but I'm the same way about brandy. You take most people, they really go for an after-dinner brandy. But me? Well, I have to admit it tastes better going down than coming up."

"I know what you mean," she said. "It's a funny thing about people."

Indeed, we had a pleasant meeting of minds there in the airplane, stacked for an hour or so over North Piddling. Though there was a pertinent point I didn't think to bring up before we landed, and it is this: When people say it is a funny thing about them, you will probably be able to control your hysterics. They are only getting ready to announce the shattering fact that they don't like something. And it's not going to be something that's really quite awful, like suttee or apartheid; it's going to be something small.

Oh, once in a long while, to be sure, the phrase will precede the simple declaration of a fascinating personal idiosyncrasy (it's a funny thing about me; peanut butter always cures my hiccups), delivered with the same modest pride with which one admits to not being able to read his own handwriting. But you don't run into these variations quite so often, so I guess they're not quite so funny.

No, dislikes are more stimulating, apparently, than devotions. I believe it was William James who said that Damn braces, Bless relaxes.* And, indeed, I found this out after I wrote *The I Hate to Cook Book*. People suggested all manner of similar follow-ups, from *I Hate to Garden* to an

* It's not only that I believe William James said it, I'm sure he did. But I've learned that inserting a fact that way isn't so flat-footed, sometimes, as starting right out with "So-and-So said. . . ." It just seems to make the sentence read a little better.

in-depth study of the Rockettes on strike, *I Hate to Kick*. But as it happened, I didn't possess enough interior knowledge of these things to hate them properly. So I eventually settled for *I Hate to Housekeep*, having always considered housekeeping rather a dusty bore, stuffed as it is with small necessary unimportances, to borrow Maggie Rennert's good phrase, and most of the existing literature about it seemed so full of advice no one in her right mind would ever take.[1]

However, everyone needs a garden of aversions to wander around in now and again, for it helps channel the venom away from where it doesn't belong.

A woman told me that when she gets mad at her family, she tries to deflect it to the movie-house people who put the word Adult on their marquees when they mean pornographic or scatological. Then, after she's hated them for a while, she bears down on—for instance—the newscasters who say "A large amount of people." Because "amount" is for inanimate, not animate, objects. Why depersonalize us any further? you can hear her scream, nearly any evening when the wind is right.

The other night, at a party, the hostess distributed pencils and paper during the grim digestive period after dinner, and we played a List Game. Everyone listed, in anonymous block-print letters, ten things he hated. Then the lists were shuffled and read aloud, and we tried to match them to the guests.

No one guessed mine (which included List Games, Bartók, Creole food, denture-cream commercials that glue the lead pencil to a long prehensile forefinger, Kabuki dancers, Old-Fashioned glasses that look like soup cans, Volendam, and Euclid Avenue), and it's no wonder, because I had included some of them to sound more knowledgeable than I am, not because they really bother me much.

But that night I couldn't stop thinking about them as I was going to sleep—about the sand in the daily machinery, the flies in the rice pudding (and it's a funny thing about me, I don't like the rice pudding much better than I like the flies).

In they swarmed. Tiny rosebud-shaped soaplets. Envelopes marked OCCUPANT, URGENT, from Kansas City insurance companies. Cardboard ads telling me I may have already won my $50,000 Dream Home, bound into a magazine so I can't fold it back.

Coffee cups shallow as soup plates.
Sea food in barbecue sauce.
Anything served flaming.
Garter belts.
Daylight-saving time.
Female harmony trios.
Making telephone calls.
Afternoons.
Ms. meaning Mrs. or Miss. (Ms. is Manuscript.)
Bare feet, except on babies.
Playboy Clubs.
Patterned bathroom tissue.
Foam-rubber bed pillows.
Corpse-type lipstick.
Transparent pocketbooks.

And the Beautiful People. And the people who write about the Beautiful People. And the people who don't sound the final s in vichyssoise. And the people who say "nauseous" when they mean "nauseated." And the people who say "I could care less" when they mean "I couldn't care less." And the people who say "Bye now" or "Bye-bye" or "Nighty-noodles." And the people who say "Drinky-poo." And the people who drink so many drinky-poos they can't talk straight and won't quit talking either.

And washcloths thick as carpets, so you can't feel your face through them and tell where you've washed.

And social teas.

And watching pro football.

And washing salad greens.

And listening to little children tell the plots of books or movies. Or to grownups ditto.

And making between-the-acts conversation at the theater.

And gas-station gambling games.

And wrapping up gifts.

And good recipes on packages that you come to depend on, and then they change the package and omit the recipe.

And reading first-person-female novels by male writers and vice versa, because no matter how good they are I don't believe them.

And pages of dialogue without any "he said"s, so one must backtrack painfully with the forefinger.

And all holidays. (One day a year we should have an egg hunt in the morning, firecrackers with a turkey lunch, and a Christmas present all around before bedtime.)

And sweaty team games, because I was early traumatized by the gummy bindings on the high-school hockey sticks and the hammy thighs of the girl who was in love with the gym teacher. Indeed, all group sweat sports, as distinguished from blood sports, which I hate, too.

There they were, heaping the bedclothes, all these little things I can't stand. It was a wholesome exercise in unbridled petulance, I thought as I changed the sheets the next day, and I recommend it for the quick temporary relief of minor aches and tensions caused by looking around.

Still, it didn't quite go to the heart of the matter, as I realized presently, for I kept thinking about Hates. And thus it came to me the following morning, with some surprise, that what I actually hate the most is Sin.[2]

Sin bothers me considerably and always has, perhaps because my maternal grandfather was a Presbyterian minister. It was from him, perhaps, that I inherited a conscience that's studded with shoulds and shouldn'ts like a clove-stuck ham, making me feel bad both before and after I've done something, though fortunately not while I'm doing it.

What happened, that particular morning, was this: straightening the living room and blowing the dust off the books, I came across our large family Bible, which tends to collect a good deal. And when it fell open to the Ten Commandments, I had the feeling somebody was trying to tell me something. Then I realized that it was the Sabbath and I shouldn't be working. I sat down.

Presently, as I reread the Ten—it had been years since our paths had crossed—I was astonished at the leeway they allow. For without breaking a one, of course, you can pull the wings off robins, kick old ladies (just so one of them isn't your own), burn books, ban books, set up a ghetto and run a slum, persecute anybody, buy votes to get elected Grand Kleagle, sell submachine guns to morons, work your children in the mines from 7:00 A.M. to midnight or chain them in the basement, cut down redwoods for firewood, dump all Boston's garbage into Walden Pond, stay dead drunk or blow your skull on your choice of poison, and in general have a high old time, just so you don't do it on Sunday. Clearly, the Ten were only for openers.

OO Then as I studied the problem further, I didn't think the Seven Deadly Sins were holding up much better. For it seemed to me there is hardly a one we could do without. . . . *I.e.,* if I hadn't envied my neighbor his watertight roof, my own would still leak, and the children would catch cold. And we need Avarice, with taxes the mess they are, for you must want more in order to get more, and you'd better get more unless you want Big Daddy to take ultimate care of you—see Pride. And without Lust we wouldn't be here discussing it. And so on.

It is no wonder that the positive "Love thy neighbor as thyself" looked really splendid, till it became clear that we don't like ourselves intelligently enough yet to make it work.

And equally splendid is the commandment "Thou shalt love the Lord thy God with all thy heart and with all thy soul and with all thy mind," except that such a mountain of trouble has been made by people who thought they were doing so. It is a difficult subject, and good men do not agree.

So it seemed to me time—for myself, at any rate—to regress: to go from the simplistic back to the detailed, in keeping with these more complicated times. When in doubt, spell it out. And when I read, only a few nights later, about the Buddhists who do just that, with their own roster of 108 sins,[3] for which they bong the temple bell 108 times every New Year's Eve, I was delighted. This, I felt, is the kind of check list everyone needs, nowadays, for his own personal reference. I would have my own roster, too. . . . As of course anyone can, though I warn you that both the compiling and the testing take time.

The article I read didn't say what theirs were, which was just as well; I'd have been diffident about compiling my own. As it was, I had a clear field.

And yet, as I say, it wasn't easy. First, there was the way a sin can ooze into a stupidity: where does one become the other? Then, I was aware that I had committed, or been involved in committing, most of them, with only an embarrassingly few exceptions, which didn't make it easier.

And what about the sins that aren't sinful all the time—

the Moot Sins? Number 5, for example, wouldn't be a sin in a boys' dorm, nor would Number 29, the first time, because you have to find out somehow. Nor would Number 39, if it simply can't be helped, nor Number 50, if one has some crippling disease of the hands.

Indeed, I think this was one reason my grandfather finally left the ministry for the mortgage business, though I suspect that my grandmother's attitude might have had something to do with it, too. (She sometimes ended her prayers with "And if you'll just tend to Your business, Lord, I'll tend to mine," apparently feeling that things went along all right except when the Lord decided to stick his nose into them.)

Some of these 108 are, of course, bigger than others. Also, one probably gets more points for resisting those that are especially appealing. I've never had trouble resisting Numbers 43 or 52 or 18, for example—just not inclined that way—but 54, say, is a different matter.

And I'd like to point out that 108 sins is a lot of sins, not something you can toss off before breakfast. I was tempted, at times, to do as Charles Schulz's Lucy did, padding out her *Peter Rabbit* book report: "And so Peter Rabbit busted into Mr. MacGregor's garden and stole some parsley and some asparagus and some turnips and some carrots and some chard and some beets and some kohlrabi . . ." which gives you a fast seven sins for one.

But I didn't, except in a few cases. Therefore, most of them cover considerable ground. I have explained the ones that I thought might need explaining, for I want to be as co-operative as I can. Though I didn't come here to argue.

The 108

1. Leaving a mess behind you.
2. Pretending to know what you do not know.

3. Telling someone something unpleasant someone else said about him unless you think his knowing it is vital to his pursuit of happiness. Once I knew a parrot who would bite you on the ankle and say Ouch.
4. Forcing someone to have another helping when he doesn't want another helping.
5. Not putting the seat down on the toilet.
6. Pretending affection you don't feel (not only sinful but dangerous, for one day they'll try to redeem your paper money).
7. Naming your child after you, which can give him the feeling he's got too tough an act to follow.
8. Not saying "I don't agree with you," and why, when it's a matter worth taking a stand on, unless it's some jackass who wouldn't understand you if you talked all night.
9. Poking hungrily, unasked, into someone's psyche. (It is better to accept the façade, for most of us go to great trouble building and maintaining one, punctually changing the goodies in the shop window, and so on, and therefore it's a great waste not to close an eye and enjoy it. Moreover, it probably contains considerable truth—at least, this is what he'd like to be, and maybe he'll make it, someday.)
10. Mentally stripping to the buff in front of anyone except a doctor, who is paid to watch and listen (for a bit of fiction protects any relationship, the way Pliofilm keeps the flies off the pie).
11. ʘʘ Bringing a baby to any public performance other than a bagpipe concert.

12. Thinking you must make the most of every golden moment and acting accordingly, unless you do so in private, for the contrast could be quite discouraging to someone who is having a bad day. (As one Boy Scout asked another, "Don't you ever have days when you feel just a little untrustworthy, disloyal, unhelpful, unfriendly, discourteous, unkind, grumpy, wasteful, cowardly, dirty, and irreverent?")
13. Not helping someone in physical or emotional distress if you know a possible way.
14. Not screwing the top securely back onto the salt shaker.
15. Giving joke presents done up to look marvelous. Last Christmas I opened a stunning satin-papered beribboned box and found, therein, my old dried-up fountain pen that had fallen out of my handbag once, in her house. Next Christmas I am going to give her short shrift. In a box. Gift-wrapped.
16. Being too positive your way is the only way.[4] I used to be like that till I became humble. Now I think I'm probably the most humble person in the entire world, and with plenty to be humble about, too, and I think people who aren't humble are perfectly stinking. They think they're so darned smart.
17. Yielding to the acid enjoyments of being malicious, unless you're so good at it that it becomes an art form, as the Alexanders Pope and Woollcott were, or Alice Roosevelt Longworth.

About the only way to resist these little pleasures is to do something rather nice for the person or group one feels malicious about, so that even he or it is bathed in the warm glow. Or so I've found it. I realize that this admission will probably gravel certain people, that is, people for whom I've done rather nice things. But they're greatly outnumbered by people I've never done anything for, who should accordingly feel pretty good.[5]

18. Automatically voting a straight ticket.

19. Stealing.

20. Making it felt when one wakes up bad-tempered, for the widening ripples can reach into the next county.

21. ʘʘ Putting fruit centers in chocolates. Fruit belongs in the fruit bowl, just as tropical fish belong in the tropics, and leopard skins on leopards (not on ladies), and zebra skins on zebras (not on floors).

22. Accepting praise for work you didn't do.

23. Holding a social grudge beyond the statute of limitations.

24. Giving a little kid who'd like to learn how to paint a canvas with all the sections numbered for proper color. Or giving a would-be sculptor a kit containing Head to be Filled in with Clay Plus Sculpting Tools and Tube of Patina for Rich Bronze Color.

25. Repeating the tag line of a joke, so people must laugh again with the old laughter stale in the mouth.

26. Fingernail biting or toenail biting. My doctor has a contortionist patient who does both, and he says you never saw such a mess.

27. Believing that everything is your fault or problem, which only creates another problem and is quite

as vain as believing that every good development was your doing.

28. Not valuing one's self enough, which seems to cause more painful fallout than valuing one's self too much, which at least provides comedy relief.
29. Hang-overs, from too much anything.
30. Not listening at least once when someone tries to tell you something he considers important.
31. Being more than fifteen minutes late for a social or business appointment. (Once I wrote an etiquette book that said twenty, but I am older now and crosser.)
32. Discussing a spouse's shortcomings with an eager friend. (I'll trade you a juicy fault of my husband's for one of your husband's, and eventually we'll have both marriages shot down over the coffee break.)
33. Reading someone else's diary or letters unless it's Samuel Pepys's or.Lady Mary Wortley Montagu's or St. Paul's, and so on.
34. Digging inside the ear with the finger and examining with prolonged dispassionate interest whatever was removed.
35. Unloading one's own shabby prejudices on children.
36. Not working a good part of the time, for this can lead to peckishness.
37. Not letting someone else work, for this can lead to mayhem.
38. Withering a newborn idea with a laugh or a look.

39. Having more than two and one-half children, or, neater still, two.

40. Not showing a little courage when the occasion demands and exhibiting damn-fool bravado when there's no demand at all.

41. Announcing a fine intention and relaxing permanently in the glow of having announced it.

42. Hiring an expensive expert for his expertise but getting your pound of flesh by preventing him from doing an expert's job through your eagerness to prove you're not so dumb yourself.

43. Spitting in the street (or in the living room, for that matter, or anywhere except in a cow pasture or a bathroom or into a handkerchief).

44. Minding other people's business, unless one's own is so ineffably dull that there's no alternative.

45. Lumping people together.[6]

46. Killing anyone.

47. ʘʘ Making someone live longer than he wants to.

48. Looking worse than you have to, if there is anyone around to look.

49. Telling someone it won't hurt when it will. Before I had had a baby, I wondered if it would hurt; and an experienced mother told me she'd rather have a baby, any time, than go to the dentist. May I meet her with one tooth in her head and it aching.

    Doctors frequently weasel this one with the word "discomfort." When a doctor says, "You may feel a little discomfort," be prepared to go straight through his acoustical ceiling. (Never trust a doctor with an acoustical ceiling.) But had he said, "This is probably going to hurt quite a lot," you could have gathered your starch together and your dignity around you.

50. Writing illegibly.
51. Rhyming words like "blue" and "blew" or "dreams" and "beans" in the fond belief that they rhyme.
52. Being possessive with someone you think you love.
53. Reading or talking or thinking too much at the fourth-grade level if one is at the fifth-grade level or at the junior level if one is at the senior level.
54. Being too pleased with one's self for a generous act that was no skin off one's nose.
55. Wanting too much to be liked at the cost of saying or doing what one really dislikes.
56. Not valuing something enough because it is yours.
57. Overvaluing it for the same reason.
58. Assuming someone is less worthy than you before he has conclusively proved it.
59. Wearing the rattiest clothes in the group because everyone knows you could wear the most expensive ones.
60. Laughing at someone if he doesn't know why, and often if he does.
61. Antiabortion laws.
62. Creating unnecessary pain.
63. If you happen to create some anyway, enjoying it.
64. Shutting the mind to something before you try it or try to understand it.

65. OO Giving people advice when they want only sympathy.[7]

66. Purposely making something ugly out of what was attractive to begin with. (Purposely is the operative word. I have knitted ugly dishrags out of attractive yarn, just as Mary Quant has messed up a lot of pretty fabric, but I'm sure we didn't mean to.)

67. Letting a talent die of neglect or cavalier treatment.

68. Pandering too much to people's shoddier impulses.

69. Telling people they can at least be clean when they don't even have enough to eat.

70. Spoiling something good with an oversell.

71. Persuading someone into your own bad habits.

72. Asking idiot questions.

    Like "Why don't you have any children?" or "Why aren't you married yet?" Or the TV newsman's favorite, "And just how did you feel, Mrs. Jones, as you watched the moving van run over your little boy?"

    Then there is "Are you sure you didn't go to any trouble?," after you *did* go to a lot of trouble but weren't going to embarrass anyone by saying so, and you know they know you did, too.

    Or "Aren't you *darling!*" I've never been able to think of a satisfactory reply to "Aren't you darling." (That is actually a peccadillo, not a grade-A sin, but it's still a no-no.)

73. Being so brave people choke on the pity they're full of and don't know what to do with. (It's sometimes more gallant to cry a little.)

74. Taking away someone's spouse, unless it is a real rescue mission (see Sin Number 13).

75. Automatically blaming someone for his grandfather's dirty work.[8]

76. Putting your face too close to another's when talking, except in bed.

77. ʘʘ Refilling someone's half-empty drink.

78. Embarrassing people with unnecessarily intimate advertising for necessarily intimate products, or with 100% dubious jokes unless one is 100% sure of the audience.

79. The millionaire's oil-depletion allowance, unless there is, equally, an idea-depletion allowance for sculptors, painters, writers, gagmen, designers, composers, and fifty other kinds of craftsmen whose livelihood depends on the finite supply of what they can drill out of their skulls.

80. Making a speech longer than forty minutes.

81. Making cocktail napkins out of Matisse or powder-room wallpaper out of Utrillo. Or background music out of Brahms, unless you are doing something rather majestic.

82. Hurting animals, whether it's wounding fawns with a bow and arrow, or overfeeding poodles, or stripping the wings from butterflies, or by whatever system.[9]

83. Banning books or burning books.

84. Grabbing the biggest piece of fudge.

85. Double-parking on Main Street.

86. Cutting down one's spouse in public; this should always be done in private.

87. Profiting from someone's grief.

88. Paying anyone else less than a white man for precisely the same work.

89. Pouring cheap liquor from lordly bottles.

90. Manufacturing or installing the kind of fluorescent lights that make people look more frayed or apoplectic than they actually are.

91. ʘʘ Borrowing a 6¢ stamp and repaying it with 6¢ instead of a stamp.

92. Preventing anyone from growing up.

93. Lying that hurts someone.

94. Spoiling something that belongs to someone else.

95. Not pulling over if you are creeping along a curly road admiring the scenery, to the mortal exasperation of drivers behind you.

96. Assuming squatters' rights on a life just because you started it or saved it or married into it.

97. Giving a gift below one's own taste level to someone, even if it's above theirs (that is, foisting something you wouldn't have in your own home onto theirs).

98. Acting morally superior toward someone busily sinning in some fashion that doesn't happen to tempt you, or which you haven't been caught at yet.

99. Spoiling someone's pleasure in something he thinks is great, which you know is awful, if you needn't live with it or suffer through it.

100. Turning a reputable valley into a disreputable car dump, or a respectable bourbon bottle into an unrespectable lamp.

101. Believing that the nightly newscast reflects the whole world as it is, and despairing accordingly. In an earlier day, it was taught that man must have a "full despising of himself," which he can achieve easily any evening, just watching the news. But this has proved to be dangerous. As with a little child who is told again and again that he is stupid, he is ugly, he is wicked, too many negative neutrons can be activated.[10]

    Therefore one must make a point of remembering, often unassisted, that uncounted millions of good people are still minding the store: Working around the clock to solve immense problems and little ones, or heroically tending their own gardens, or with great patience and sense helping other people tend theirs, or going one more round when they're positive they can't, or showing enduring fortitude in the face of dullness, going home when they'd rather not go home, or not going home when they'd rather go home, but going on, instead to sit on a hard chair in an endless meeting that may or may not help solve the sanitation problem for the north end of town, which is full of civilization's dropouts who threw up their hands after seeing too many nightly newscasts.

102. Not taking care of a plant or animal given to you.
103. Giving someone a plant or animal he doesn't want.
104. Hitting someone smaller, hard.
105. Lying to one's self even more than one has to.
106. ʘʘ Putting tomatoes in clam chowder.
107. Complaining about something like 106 when there are so many better things to pick on.

108. For the life of me I couldn't think of the 108th sin. But I'm not going to worry about it now, for, like cable cars, there's always another if you look, just visible over the hill.

NOTES

1. "Don't toss out those Sherman Tank thrust bearings! Weld them on the ends of 1936 Oakland camshafts wrapped with 5,000 feet of old transatlantic cable stripped of insulation. Bolt on two old seventy-five-pound mushroom anchors, and you have a couple of fine revolving outdoor patio lamp-post barbecue grills!"

—DEREK WILLIAMSON

2. "It's odd how we feel impelled to react to everything in moral terms. Why does *everything* have to seem good or bad to us? Particularly when we know that whatever we now think good we shall eventually think bad, and vice versa. We're like tossed pennies, that can register nothing but heads or tails. Good God, is there no aspect of the universe that we don't feel compelled either to encourage or discourage with our little smiles and frowns? Let us put ten minutes aside each day to practice feeling morally numb."

—MICHAEL FRAYN

3. " 'We Buddhists believe there are 108 sins of mankind,' said the Reverend Keiseki Yamasato, pastor of the Hongwanji Buddhist Mission. 'At midnight on the New Year we strike the bell once for each sin.' He said the ceremony takes twenty minutes to half an hour because when the bell is struck the sound is allowed to die away completely before the bell is struck again. During the ceremony the mallet is passed from hand to hand. 'Sometimes 12 men come at midnight to ring the bell,' said the Reverend Yamasato."

—The Honolulu *Advertiser*

4. ". . . It is an unobtrusive little vice which she shares with nearly all women who have grown up in an intelligent

circle united by a clearly defined belief; and it consists in a quite untroubled assumption that the outsiders who do not share this belief are really too stupid and ridiculous. . . . It is not, in fact, very different from the conviction she would have felt at the age of ten that the kind of fish-knives used in her father's house were the proper or normal or 'real' kind, while those of the neighboring families were 'not real fish-knives' at all."

—C. S. LEWIS, *The Screwtape Letters*

5. " 'Be you spited at me?' asks the Pennsylvania Dutch housewife timidly. 'Spited I ain't,' answers the woman at the ironing board. 'But so Christian as I should oderwise feel, I don't.' "

—*Papa Is All*

6. ". . . You take their faces away from 'em by calling them masses, and then you accuse 'em of not having any faces. To me there are still just a lot of people about—too many, perhaps, and too much alike nowadays—but still people, not masses. The back street I grew up in might look to an outsider like a typical warren of the masses, but it didn't look to me like that, because I knew the people and they were all different."

—J. B. PRIESTLEY

7. "If there is one thing I can't stand, it's constructive criticism."

—DR. LINUS ZICKENING

8. "Talk about three hundred years of slavery and oppression doesn't stir—in me—any feeling of racial culpability. I want to be honored with a personal indictment, and perhaps have earned it, but if an angry man attacks me on

some black street, it will be the absurd murder of someone who is being tried but does not yet feel convicted."

—PETER SCHRAG

9. ". . . I share mammalian characters with a small mouse who inhabits my desk drawer. This is hard to account for in a disordered world, so that recently, when I came upon this mouse, trapped and terrified in the wastebasket, his similarity to myself rendered me helpless, and out of sheer embarrassment I connived his escape."

—LOREN EISELEY

10. "Someone said when willpower and imagination lead in two different directions, imagination will always win. Imagination is more powerful than sheer willpower. Therefore, to have a high image of what man is to become and concentrate one's attention upon it is to move toward it almost automatically; but to spend all one's time fighting against the evil impulses is to keep one's mind so much upon them that they have a better chance to get hold of one. What gets your attention gets *you,* finally."

—G. ARTHUR CASADAY

PART TWO

The Mal-de-Merry-Go-Round

CHAPTER FIVE

*

Who, Me?

" 'I, A Woman' has refreshing appeal because its central figure is a girl who cheerfully accepts sexual adventures with a delighted good-humor.

"Throughout various encounters, she is playful, independent and enticing. And so she remains, unconquered, without remorse or guilt: an extremely attractive woman.

"She is often without clothes, in fact, she strips with pleasure . . . but the case is handled with taste and objectivity, and the cast are both skilled and likable."

—PAINE KNICKERBOCKER,
The San Francisco *Chronicle*

AT BREAKFAST THE OTHER DAY I WAS POURing the coffee when Mr. Knickerbocker's review in the morning paper happened to catch my eye.

"Thunder Turtles!" I gasped, for I had been rereading *Little Men* the night before.

"What? Want some cereal?" my husband asked, waving the Sludgie box around. We're a Sludgie family; don't eat the Breakfast of Champions; just a bunch of middle-achievers around here.

"Sure," I said, accepting the Sludgies with a delighted good humor, and then I started reading the *I, A Woman* review aloud.

"Whockets!" exclaimed my husband, joining in, reading over my shoulder. " 'She is often without clothes, in fact, she strips with pleasure. . . .' " He eyed me narrowly. "You've got your clothes on again."

"I can't help it, it's cold in here," I said. "Anyway, you're a great one to talk. Remember yesterday afternoon."

He had the grace to blush. Susan Scrimshaw, from across the street, had brought her portable radio over to see if he could fix it, and while he brought his tools out to the front stoop, I trotted down to the post office. Well, when I got back home, there they both were, still on the front stoop, hadn't fixed a thing besides the radio.

"And after all the John O'Hara you've read!" I said now. "All the John D. MacDonald! All the . . ." But he'd already slunk off to his workshop, properly embarrassed.

So I settled down to my grocery list. I wanted some of that Mouthwash for Lovers, in case somebody dropped by, and I also needed some more bourbon and vodka, because Susan's brother is back home now, just out of college, and I know it takes real effort these days to entertain a graduate.

My little girl came into the breakfast room then. "Rotten rainy old Saturday," she said, looking with distaste out the window. "What'll I do, Mommie?"

"Why don't you practice your guitar?" I suggested.

"I already did," she said.

"Or see if Jennifer can come over and play," I said. Jennifer is the only other eleven-year-old around.

"She's at her grandma's," my little girl said.

"Then read awhile. I have to finish my grocery list and pick up Florence Heflinger and go to the store," I said. (The neighbors' car was on the blink again.)

"Okay," she said, with resignation, and was presently curled on the sofa by the fire, deep in a book.

It wasn't long before I'd done the dishes, put on my raincoat, and found the car keys. I was just starting out to the garage when she called to me. "Hey, Mom, what's a pederast?"

"Gosh, honey, I don't know," I said, embarrassed at my stupidity. But there are so many of those words around now that I have a hard time keeping them straight. "I'm afraid you'll have to look it up, dear, okay?" And as I drove up the Heflingers' driveway I was thinking, Oh my, what a lot the little ones have to learn nowadays!

Just then Jill Heflinger plunged out and headed across the street lugging her guitar and a transistor radio. I guess she didn't see me through her hair. Jill is fourteen and takes her teen-age responsibilities very hard, looking as funny as any of them, and knowing the rock groups apart, and keeping up with the current literature and the movies.

Then her mother came out, and I don't know when I've seen Florence Heflinger so upset.

"Honestly!" she said, lighting the wrong end of a filter-tip as she settled herself in the front seat. "I mean, *really!*"

"What's the matter, Flo?" I asked, as I headed for the store.

"Jill called me a hypocrite, because she's going out with the Scrimshaw boy tonight and I said she had to be back home by eleven o'clock." Then Flo told me about the rest of their conversation.

"What do you mean, 'hypocrite'?" she'd asked Jill.

"Ashly, you needn't lie to me, Mother," Jill said. "Don't think you're fooling me. I know what grownups ashly do."

"I should hope so, at your age," her mother had said.

"I don't mean like in bed, like you and Daddy," her daughter said. "I mean like affairs. *You* know. Like with other people," she explained.

Florence lit another cigarette, which made two she had going, and puffed like a choo-choo train. "But I'm not *having* any affairs," she said to me. "Where did I go wrong?"

Well, I couldn't tell her, because I've been wondering the same thing about myself. I haven't had an affair for a month of Sundays, and I'd be ashamed to face John Updike, not to mention Jackie Susann or Françoise Sagan or, well, nearly anybody else. Of course, it's true that I'm a little—well, maturer?—than some of their characters. But not all of them, not by a long shot. You can't keep Mother out of the hay any more, or Grandma in her rocker either.

I've been worried, too, about all these sex surveys and depth interviews. If they happen to call me, what can I tell them that's *significant?* Of course, you can always invent something. But you can't lie to yourself.

"Look, you've been busy," I said comfortingly, as much to myself as to Florence. "After all, with Chuck and the children and the house, and your hospital committee—"

"Not *that* busy," she said firmly, and I could see that her conscience wouldn't let her off the hook. (She's always been that type, Flo has—if she thinks she's remiss in the smallest thing, she can't sleep nights.) "In the books, they're *never* too busy," she continued doggedly. "They work it in *some* way. Like they go to a dinner party, and pretty soon the host disappears with one of the guests."

"Yes, but you know how it is around here," I said. "You go out to dinner, and the master bedroom's always full of coats, and the kids are right down the hall, or something. Don't be so hard on yourself."

She brooded in silence as I drove toward the shopping center in the rain. We were going to the Lakeshore Shopping Plaza because I had to pick up the curtains from the dry cleaner's. And I was thinking, That's another thing:

just keeping a house going takes so many pesky errands, and if you had to work an affair in around everything else, it would be just one huckleberry too much.

Still, I've always heard, if you want something done, ask the busy person to do it. You'd simply have to be efficient about it, I suppose. Get organized.

"What about a wife-swapping club?" I suggested (incidentally wondering as I mentioned it why they're always called wife-swapping clubs, never husband-swapping clubs, and what does Betty Friedan think about *that?*). Not that I know of any around here, but Flo is really up on the community doings.

"Well—" She looked dubious. "I've heard that they're awfully good now, but I don't know where they are. And it's so hard to get people together for anything these days, everyone's so busy. And another thing—" she turned to me—"you know Chuck, the way he'll never phone if he's going to be late. *I'm* used to it—you know how it is with your own husband—but somebody else's is a different kettle of clams. I mean, say we were going to get together and swap, just us two couples, and Chuck missed the 5:22, we'd all have to wait around. I think it'd be rude not to. And I know how busy *you* are, and you'd probably be miffed, and first thing you know, you'd be blaming it on *me*—"

She was right, of course. "I know," I said. "Nothing is ever as simple as it looks."

So we pulled into the supermarket parking lot and sat for a minute, waiting for the rain to ease off.

"All the same," Flo said, "I wish I could figure it out. I think those books and movies know something we don't know. Take the way they do all that drinking at the same time. Always building fresh drinks, and after six or eight they head for the bedroom wherever they are—"

"Not necessarily," I interrupted. "Anywhere is okay, as I get it."

"Wherever they are," she agreed, "and then Wow! Why, if I had that much to drink, I'd—" She stopped. "But I mean, like Saturday night. Chuck was awfully tired, and he had one Martini too many, and when we—I mean, when he—" She stopped again.

"I know," I said. "Though what impresses me most in the books is the way they talk all the while they're— Well, I mean, all those clever gags and deep philosophy and everything. I know when *my* husband and I—" I stopped. The rain had, too, so we went in, to trundle our shopping carts down the aisles.

But I could hardly keep my mind on my grocery list, for wondering about it all, and hoping along with Florence that our daughters wouldn't discover the true state of things with us. (I know mine thinks I'm square enough anyway, because I wear lipstick sometimes.)

Of course, they don't think about us too much at that, because naturally they're pretty busy thinking about sex, and bound to get busier as their sex lives develop naturally from TV sex to school-and-magazine sex to movie-and-book sex, which makes it so complicated that any average-bright girl would realize that she'd better get going on her lab work now she's done her Suggestive Reading, wouldn't she? After all, from little up, she was taught that anything worth doing is worth doing well, wasn't she? You don't wait around for Mr. Right any more; you practice up for him.

And yet, in a way, I can't help thinking with nostalgia of the good old days before Lee De Forest invented Marshall McLuhan, the good old innocent movie days before Constant Viewer had turned into Constant Voyeur, the good old rotten hypocritical literary days when novelists fell back on their asterisks, way back when people took their mouth-wash as it came, and their sex, too, and hushed up about it, and one way or another you could look your children in the eye.

Because the way things are going now, Florence and I get this feeling that everybody's out of step but us. Ashly.

SUPPLEMENTARY READING

". . . Sex, they say, must be the dominant drive in everybody's life. You would think that a casual glance at a busful of housewives—the Cabinet—the W.I.—the Rotary—would make them think twice about the idea: do they *look* as if their lives were governed by sexual passion?"

—KATHARINE WHITEHORN

"I hope you will agree with me that the NBC spectacular 'The Pursuit of Pleasure' requires the network to present the other and healthier side of the picture. Theirs was a one-sided, grotesquely distorted view of the lives of a small minority whose ideas of 'pleasure' seem to consist exclusively of sex and drugs. If, as the experts assure us, only 25 per cent of the American people have ever flown in an airplane, I believe that I would be justified in assuming that a considerably smaller percentage have seen a topless show, smoked marijuana, taken LSD, belonged to a rowdy motorcycle gang, or rolled on a tiger skin with a blonde."

—G. A. BALDWIN

CHAPTER SIX

The Knee-Jerk Consumer

"Grab a whole big bunch of it and throw it against the wall."
—ROWAN & MARTIN

THE OTHER DAY I HAD TO RUSH DOWN TO THE store to get a bottle of the new improved mouthwash, because that cute girl on the telly smashed my old kind on the floor.

"Ullllp, that old unimproved brand!" she said, and I can tell you, I was so embarrassed I nearly died.

It was a tiring trip, because I had to take an extra five minutes to fill out the Treasure Hunt map at the gas station and five more to argue with the man about the fourth salad plate in the complete dinner service I was working on before they switched promotions.

Then I tried to phone home but got the busy signal, and I knew what it was, all right. My little girl is very musical, and ever since Bat McGonegal started his "Pass the Buck" show—first one to phone in gets the price of the record—she's been on the hot line.

Sometimes I get a little upset about it, as a matter of fact, because it seems to me the kids may be getting the wrong idea. So, on the way home, I stopped in for a chat with my good friend Winifred. Winnie and I get together periodically to watch television and discuss the curious shape of the world.

"The trouble is," I said, "kids are getting too commercial-minded these days."

"I know what you mean," she sputtered, spitting dust. She'd been pasting stamps in her trading-stamp books.

"They've got to realize," I said, "that there are other things in the world besides money."

"Right!" said Winnie. "There's merchandise. Take that slick new show I saw the other day—"

"You mean the one where the contestants take shopping carts," I said, "and streak through the store to see who can grab the most stuff the fastest?"

"No, that's Hog Stampede," Winnie said. "Been on for ages. No, I mean World-wide Goody Grab. That's where they get a free shopping spree in some foreign country or other. They get some great stuff, too."

"Well, what I mean is, kids should realize it's a question of values," I said. "A question of what's important and what isn't."

"Right!" she said. "You've got to use your head. For instance, I was wasting twenty minutes a day playing Ringo Bingo—"

"Is that the one where the MC calls telephone numbers—" I began.

"That's the one," said Winnie. "But all you get is some crummy soap flakes. Whereas, if I'd used my brains I could've come out ahead with just fifteen minutes of Jingle Plunk."

"Jingle Plunk?"

"Give us a Jingle, we Plunk down the cash," she explained. "First one to phone, you know. Or I could've played Win-A-Pile. Only that's at an awkward time, because I should be out cashing in my premium coupons."

"That's something else," I said. "Premiums. Always the big giveaway, always something for nothing. But actually—"

"Actually, it's confusing," Winnie said. "I transferred my savings to Second National for the silver-plated salad servers and then switched to Confederate Savings for my electric carving knife. Only *then* I found out I'd have got a matching salad bowl if I'd stuck just one more week with Second National. You have to stay on your toes, that's all. You better tell the kids that."

I had to agree with her, I certainly should. They'll have to stay on their toes all right and they'll have to think of something intelligent to do about this mess. For all God's chillun want goodies, and some of us got goodies, and I want to give some real thought to what we're going to do about the rest of God's chillun, the minute I fill out the postage-prepaid postcard so I can be promptly notified whether I've won the romantic Tahiti Dream Vacation for Two or the big TV-console-with-stereo-and-hi-fi in the big $250,000 Lucky Sweepstakes, and I've got to get it out to the mailbox in time for the 3:30 pickup.

SUPPLEMENTARY READING

"It is strange how the moment we have reason to be dissatisfied with ourselves we are set upon by a pack of insistent, clamorous desires. Is desire somehow an expression of the centrifugal force that tears and pulls us away from an undesirable self? A gain in self-esteem reduces considerably the pull of the appetites, while a crisis in self-esteem is likely to cause a weakening or a complete breakdown of self-discipline.

"Asceticism is sometimes a deliberate effort to reverse a reaction in the chemistry of our soul: by suppressing desire we try to re-build and bolster self-esteem."

—ERIC HOFFER

"The urgent search for the vitally necessary is likely to stop once we have found something that is more or less adequate, but the search for the superfluous has no end."

—ERIC HOFFER

CHAPTER SEVEN

A Dollar Is a Sometime Thing

" 'What troubles?' asked Flora, interestedly, as she busily made fresh tea. . . . 'Haven't you enough money?' For she knew that this is what is the matter with nearly everybody over twenty-five."

—STELLA GIBBONS

A MAGAZINE EDITOR WROTE TO ME A WHILE ago, wanting to know if I would review a book for them.

"Will you do a review of Sal Nuccio's *New York Times Guide to Personal Finance*?" was the exact wording, as I remember.

It occurred to me that perhaps they were asking Willie Mays to review *The Complete Book of Home Embroidery,* too, or getting Zsa Zsa Gabor's ideas on *The Woman's Own Encyclopedia of House-cleaning Helps from Attic to Basement*. But I happened to be unusually interested in personal finance at the time, having recently been taken poor, and though book reviews don't pay very much, it's still money. So I said I would, and I did.

It was a good book, though terribly sound. And oddly pure. I got the impression that Mr. Nuccio wasn't quite leveling about some of the aspects of money that really puzzle people. I mean the itty-bitty nitty-gritty part of the thing, or about some of the low holds and dirty grips that can be so helpful in handling it. And, frankly, I am glad that he left that one little fuzzy green corner, just this side of left field, vacant for me.

Not that I blame the author for his omissions. Far from it. It is a rare expert who clearly realizes how inexpert someone else can be. Naturally, he didn't think to explain things like why your Assets and Liabilities should balance, the way they do on stockholders' reports. (If I owed precisely as much as I have, I'd know I was in terrible shape, but the corporations all brag about it.) Or whether twenty-five bobby pins for 32¢ are cheaper than thirty-five bobby pins for 43¢, though I don't actually care, because so far as I'm concerned, bobby pins went out with half-moons on fingernails.

But there are other things; things of a psychological nature.

Like, why does it hurt so much to leave a half-used 29¢ jar of mayonnaise behind in a $15.00-per-day vacation motel-room refrigerator? That is to say, it hurts me. I cannot bring myself to abandon 20¢ worth of good mayonnaise. Once, I carried a small half-full jar of it for hundreds of miles in my nice leather handbag, which has a haunting fragrance now, and a permanent bulge—carried that mayonnaise tenderly till I got back home and *then* threw it out, because, after all, it had been unrefrigerated for quite a while at that point, and you can't be too careful.

And why does my rich friend Louise balk at the price

of paper napkins, preferring to spend good time washing and ironing cloth napkins? (At our place we bring out cloth napkins only for visiting potentates, but we haven't had any yet.)

And why will I buy a bottle of good perfume as a gift without wincing, while I begrudge every red cent for fancy paper to wrap it up in?

And why does my friend Annabel squeeze her dollar bills till they resemble damp green balloons, while her checks fly about like autumn leaves?

Mr. Nuccio didn't cover these matters. On second thought, I don't think I will either. They're too personal.

The fact is, money—and how you feel about it and what you do with it—is such intimate territory that it's hard to be honest about it. Yet it's big territory. I must admit that money, or no money, is quite a part of my personal landscape, the fact of it being as all pervasive as the weather.

One day I started to count the times money entered my mind, but I had to quit, because it made me feel too crass. You're not supposed to like it, or to think about it much. Or talk about it either, so far as that goes. I have a friend who is so genteel that she'll never mention the price of anything, only its approximate cost in bottles of bourbon. "A really great dress," she'll say, "and only a six-bottle job!"

Love, work, money. Those are all good things. And, like the first two, money presents complexities that are never entirely resolved. For instance, your money, and your friends' money.

I've decided that being poorer than the people you know is a problem. So is being richer. (Having exactly the same amount isn't really a problem; it just gets dull, and there's nobody to borrow from.)

In the first instance—being poorer—you have a nagging feeling that they should spring for the check somewhat oftener than they do. Still, if they pay everything in sight, they're showing off. Therefore you dislike them either way.

In the second instance, when you are the comparatively rich one, it's dangerously easy to overcompensate: working too hard at being one of the gang, poor-mouthing it over lunch with your poor little old friends about the high cost of margarine, and it's a wonder you leave with your front teeth intact. But if, instead, you overcompensate by overspending, they are equally miffed (as we have seen in the previous paragraph), and they may revenge your affluence by not thanking you enough, or not even thanking you at all. And while you certainly didn't expect any thanks, still, all the same . . .

These are sticky wickets, and it's no wonder the rich usually marry the rich and the poor usually marry the poor and the middling usually marry the middling. The money situation is a difficult one, no two ways about it; and expense accounts probably prevent as many problems as they create, which is saying a good deal.

I believe that one's basic financial attitudes are—like a tendency toward fat knees—probably formed *in utero,* or, at the very latest, *in cribbo.* They only become more so with age. The little tightwad who won't give you a chaw of his licorice grows up into the big tightwad who won't even pull out the company credit card. The little dimwit who throws his pablum all over you whether you want it or not will throw his grown-up goodies around the same way.

I think, too, that you learn your own basic financial

facts of life about the same time as the basic other ones. In my case, both came early.

They used to launder me in the same bathtub with my brother, who was two years older. This was either to teach me penis envy or to save water, probably both. (I come from a long line of nonlotus-eaters, and they really knew how to save water.) But it didn't make me envious; complacent, rather, for I felt I was more adroitly designed than he was. Still do, in fact, though we haven't compared notes lately.

However, it was only shortly after this period that I embarked on my first business venture, a lemonade stand, which opened early one July morning and closed with finality around sundown. By noon I had gone through all the lemons in the house and made 50¢. My father said that the wise thing to do would be to sink my capital into more lemons, which I did.

But I sold no more lemonade, because by that time I'd run out of neighbors. Thus I learned never to put excess capital back into the business.

It's too bad these early lessons don't stick. A while ago, through some oversight, I had 2,000 extra dollars, and a broker bought some stock for me. Shortly afterward he notified me happily that the company was splitting shares, two for one, which meant I owned twice as much, right? And then the stock dropped like a shot goose, so I lost twice as much twice as fast, right? Still in the lemon business.

Then there was the bank failure. We had a school savings program, and I almost threw myself out of the third-grade window when the banks failed, taking my 132 pennies with them. I learned from this that you'd better spend it before someone else does, and the hell with Ben Franklin.

And yet . . . and yet . . . Well, there were my frugal genes to contend with, for I had some ancestors who squoze the nickels till the Indians war-danced. When my paternal grandfather, for instance, loaned my father $100 to get married with, he saw no sense letting sentiment interfere with business, and he charged him interest at the going bank rate. He was a crisp old cookie, my grandfather* was, and it's no wonder my grandmother sang alto.

It's all these things together, I suppose, that have made me the financial schiz I am today, one half of which doesn't know what the other half doeth and would throw up if it did.

Still, I suspect that there are several of us sorely divided folk around—lead-footed grasshoppers who would love to jump around in the sunshine spitting tobacco juice all day but can't, wholeheartedly, because we know we'd hate ourselves in the morning. At least, I've often read our contributions on the Family Page of the daily paper. . . .

HOW I SOLVED MY PROBLEM

Recently we were quite worried when we discovered that our family finances were a mess. Each month we made so many payments for our modern conveniences that it was inconvenient. We tried keeping a firm weekly budget, but this did not work. Finally, one night, we had a family conference to decide which modern conveniences we could do without. We decided we could not do without any. Then we got to thinking that everybody we knew was more or less in the same boat, and anyhow you only live once, and so . . .

And so I'd like to pass along a few contributions myself

* Kin, I think, to a man I heard about who figured that the best way to get ahead security-wise was to decrease his expenditures every time his income went up, by the same percentage. He did pretty well, and the last anyone heard, he was living in the chicken house.

—some practical pointers on staying afloat, or making it a little jollier while sinking.

For one thing, it's important to stay in funds, because being on your uppers is so much more expensive. I remember once when I was stony, the lavish life I had to lead. The corner drugstore didn't accept credit cards, so I couldn't eat there. Had to go first-class, where they *did* accept credit cards, and once you're in a decent restaurant, it's silly to order the ground round.

(Friends of mine tell me they are learning the same lesson from their boy at college. He keeps telephoning cross-country collect, because he doesn't have the price of a stamp. Thus do the generations learn from each other. Not what they're supposed to learn from each other, perhaps, but still they learn.)

In fact, having some good credit cards is more important to the financial schiz than staying in funds. Especially the generalized type of credit card, like Master Charge, or Bankamericard. Cash, of course, hurts too much to spend, while writing checks has a delayed but equally painful reaction. With checks, the trouble is that you have to fill out the check stubs with What For and How Much, or you'll be even more fouled up than you are. This can't help but remind you of what stupidity you spent it on, which can be painful, inasmuch as it's probably lost its shine or busted, or been eaten, or drunk up, or is, in one way or another, all gone. But those tactful credit-card billings seldom itemize. They just present you with the sum total, and if they do enclose any carbons of sales slips, you don't have to look at them.

However, buying things can be a real problem to the lead-footed grasshopper, involving—as it does—the hard choice of Money vs. Object.

For instance, I seldom enjoy a terribly expensive thing, because I feel so obligated toward it. (Unless it is a bathrobe; I wear bathrobes a great deal and therefore wear them out.) But I get sick of an expensive thing nearly as fast as I get sick of a cheap thing, just feel guiltier about it. So the way it works out, if you're an LFG, is that the grasshopper part of you buys things in a mad moment of abandon, and the lead feet keep you from ever doing anything intelligent about it. You're somehow duty bound to keep it somewhere, molding away.

It's true that once in a while, a clear-eyed self-catechism can help. Take the case of my Lavender Paisley Designer Culottes, a rollicking impulse buy, which sag in the rear and have inhabited the bottom drawer of my dresser through many a long bright season.

Q. Did you ever—before you owned a pair of lavender paisley culottes—reflect that if only you had a pair of LPC your life would be complete?
A. No.

Q. In other words, you felt reasonably fulfilled, so to speak, even before the lavender paisley culottes came into your life?
A. Well, yes, I guess so.

Q. And when you bought the LPC, was it because you thought, *Oh boy! Just what I need for such-and-such a purpose . . .* ?
A. No.

Q. And since you received them, have you ever found anything to wear them to?
A. No.

Q. No dogfights, no grunion runs?
A. No.

Q. And you don't know any nearsighted ladies who sag in the rear and would enjoy owning a pair of LPC?

A. No.

Q. Then wouldn't it be sensible to place them in the Out file?

I forget what I answered to that one. All I know is that I still have the culottes.

The trouble is, the two sides of our nature are in a state of constant warfare, and war is always expensive. Only the other day I learned this anew, when I got a $2.00 ticket for overparking, because I was in a shop buying a non-returnable Sale Sweater there wasn't time to try on in my panic to get back to the car to avoid a parking ticket. However, I reminded myself, it would have cost me $2.00 to park in a lot anyhow. Shucks, the way things are going, make it $2.50. So I had really made 50¢, which I applied on the price of the other sweater I had to buy because the Sale Sweater didn't fit, as I found when I got it home.

But let's look now at the brighter side of bill paying, which is something else the Personal Finance Guide didn't mention except to talk about budgets, wouldn't you know?

There are a number of things you can do when the bills come in, besides cry. For one, you can fill in the blank supplied for Amount Enclosed (with $40.00 or whatever the sum is that you're going to enclose) and then forget to enclose it. If the company has any decency, it won't put you in jail, it will only send you a reasonably polite notice, saying you forgot to enclose check; and by then maybe you will have the $40.00.

This is similar in theory to mixing up your checks, which is a good system, too, when the chips and the bank balance are down. You put the correct checks in the wrong envelopes and mail them. By the time the computers stop screaming and chewing up their transistors and finally send the checks back, you may have enough money in the bank to cover them. Then you can send them out again, this time to the right places.

Too, I've found it sound practice to pay certain bills twice, when I have the scratch—not the doctor's, unless you've got something chronic and want to keep a nice little credit there, but some place where it's fun to shop. Then you have a drawing account that's pleasant to think about on rainy days.

It's even better if you can forget which store it is. Once I had a $32.00 credit because I paid twice at Kauffman's. But I got mixed up, and—thinking it was Mayer's—bought $32.00's worth of something from Mayer's that I wouldn't otherwise have bought; and when they sent me a bill for it, it rather rattled my slats. Still, I liked what I got (a nice bathrobe, as I remember) and managed to pay for it, one way or another, and I still had a pleasant slush fund waiting for me at the other place.

Then, speaking of surprises, you can prepare pleasant ones for yourself by cheating on your check stubs. Whenever you make out a check for an odd amount, say $7.19, enter it as a lavish $8.00. If you make out enough scrappy little checks during the month, a nice bonus is sure to pile up, good as found money.

However, the most important thing about money is attitude. A thing to beware of—I've noticed this frequently—is getting too much respect for money, so that you can't enjoy it informally any more.

This is easy to do, all right. If you have only one dime, you see, it's hardly worth being stingy with, let alone respectful about. You can just have fun with it, at least a dime's worth. But if you possess several dimes instead of just one, they're harder to have fun with, because larger issues are involved. A dime is no longer a plaything, like, say, a playful calf. No, it bears within it the possibilities of becoming a milch cow.

And so, should this aspect of the dime become paramount to your mind, you won't enjoy playing with it; you'll simply hate to lose it or give it away. Because, once you've acquired a whole milch cow, you think, How nice to have a herd of them!

Thus, all dimes become potential breeders instead of negotiable currency. Naturally, then, it is harder for the rich to be generous than for the poor, because it is harder to give away a cow than a drop of milk (though they may sometimes give away a whole herd if it's tax deductible).

However, the rich quite often feel terribly poor, because there are always more herds in the distance. The rich usually become constipated, too. The road to the seat in the Stock Exchange is slippery with mineral oil.

Then, another factor can enter the picture: the more money you get, the more you tend to admire your competence and doggedness for getting it (even though you merely fell over a pile of it somewhere), and your judgment of another person becomes more rigorous. Why couldn't *he* have fallen over a pile of it, too? This attitude can make people singularly unpalatable.

I'd like to make it clear, in case I haven't already, that I don't know very much about money. I've never been rich, only felt rich. I don't mean all that stuff about being healthy (which makes you feel healthy) or loved (which makes you feel loved); I mean rich.

It's all right with me, not being rich. In fact, as a freelance writer who never expected to sell anything, I was surprised at the first drop of gravy. (I've always heard, by the way, of how big that first check looks to the budding writer. That first check I got, the two-dollar check, looked exactly like $2.00.)

I was, as I say, surprised, and also interested, and I kept on writing and eventually I sold quite a lot of things. Notice, I say "sold." I never sent anything to the small inscrutable places that don't pay, partly because I didn't think I was their cuppa, but mainly because I could always hear in the far reaches of my mind my old daddy's parting words, "Dinna give it away, lass," and I never did.

And so, all that time, I felt—if not rich—fed. It was after I wrote *The I Hate to Cook Book* that I felt rich for a little while, because it began selling what seemed like an astonishing number of copies. There I was, Charlotte-off-the-yacht, the big sack of peanuts, please, and keep the change. It didn't last long because the government took such an astonishing whack of the royalties. *Sic transit, sic transit* . . .

Actually, there are only three things about money that I am reasonably sure of.

One is that having money is warming and not having money is chilling, although it is more stimulating, because you have to do something about it; and he who cuts his own wood warms himself twice.

The second thing is that you can probably save enough or gather enough together—somehow—to get what you really want, if you'll forget about what people think you ought to want. This is admittedly a depressing thought, because it means no more muddling around, Mabel, pull up your socks and make up your mind.

The remaining thing is that when you spend money, it generally isn't there any more, and you must go earn some or get somebody to give you some.

QUESTIONS & TOPICS FOR DISCUSSION

1. Why does a slight tax increase cost you $200 and a substantial tax cut save you 30¢?

2. Why are Budget Payments the ones that are the hardest on your Budget? Explain.

3. If you borrow $20,000 for twenty years at 6%, have you paid $14,389.60 on interest alone at the end of the twenty years?

Have you *really*?

4. If you put two beans in a jar on the first day, four on the second, eight on the third, and so on, and the jar is full on the thirtieth day, on what day was it half full?
(Perhaps your answer to this question—the correct answer is in the Appendix—should determine whether or not you should keep your money in a pig bank or a big bank.)

THINGS TO MAKE & DO

1. Take your age. Multiply it by two. Add five. Multiply by fifty. Subtract 365 and add the loose change in your pocket under a dollar. Now add 115.

If you did the arithmetic right, the first two figures in the answer are your age, unless you lied about it, and the last two are the change in your pocket.

It's easier, though, just to remember your age, and count your change.

CONSUMER QUIZ

1. Is a woman's half size the same as a big fat size? How come?

2. Why is it fun to buy shoes?
 ——Because your feet don't change size?
 ——Because you have a nice man right there at your feet?
 ——Because you don't have to hold your stomach in?

3. If you have a can opener that works well and a knife sharpener that works well and someone gives you a can opener that sharpens knives, too, what should you do with it?

4. If you are well supplied with salt shakers and pepper shakers and someone gives you a Pepsal, which combines the two, what should you do with it?

5. What is a Decorator Color?

6. What is a Designer Chair?

7. What is a Quality Appointment?

8. Does a flashy convertible really represent a mistress to a man?

9. What does it represent to a woman?

10. Who says so?

"The money's always useful."

—Mrs. Maude Harrison, wife of the 338,356th football-pool winner

"Poor people always lean forward when they speak because they want people to listen to them. Rich people can sit back."

—Film actor MICHAEL CAINE

"The poor like to imagine that the rich are unhappy, and here, it must be admitted, Mr. Getty's somewhat woebegone appearance is a great help.—In actual fact, to judge from his writings and one evening spent in his company, he positively likes being rich and shows no inclination, like some millionaires, to try to reconcile others to his superior financial position by engaging in public breast-beating."

—MALCOLM MUGGERIDGE

"It's our own money and we're free to spend it any way we please. It's part of this campaign business. If you have money, you spend it to win. And the more you can afford, the more you'll spend. It's something that is not regulated. Therefore, it's not unethical."

—MRS. JOSEPH P. KENNEDY

"I have found that the more money the average educated person has, then the nicer he is as an individual."

—MISS OLGA DETERDING

"Never make the unpardonable error, then, of thinking that it is romantic to be poor. For youth, which has the riches of health, it is less important; but for age, which has lost them, it is all-essential to compensate with artificial riches."

—CAITLIN THOMAS

"All I want is enough money not to have to think about it."

—RANDALL JARRELL

CHAPTER EIGHT

Don't Trust Anybody over Fifteen or Talk to Anybody under Forty

ONCE UPON A TIME THERE WAS A LITTLE BOY who was walking with his father. When they passed a funny-looking dump truck, he said, "What's that, Daddy?"

"I don't know," his father said.

Then they came to a big brick warehouse. "What's in there, Daddy?" asked the little boy.

"I don't know," his father said.

Then they saw a man doing something to the high-voltage wire on a telephone pole.

"What's that man doing, Daddy?" the little boy asked.

"I don't know," his father said.

"Daddy," said the little boy finally, "do you mind me asking you so many questions?"

"Not at all, son," said his dad. "How else are you going to learn anything?"

Or maybe it goes like this:

"Can I give Ralph the chicken bones, Mommie?" asks the little one.

"No, they're bad for dogs," says Mommie.

"Why?"

"It's like giving him a handful of needles. They splinter," Mommie explains. "And don't ever give him a pork-chop bone either; they're terrible."

Or wait a minute, is it pork chops? she thinks to herself. *Lamb chops, maybe. Veal chops? Some kind of chops anyway. Oh, well . . .*

And it is thus that knowledge flickers fuzzily from one generation to another, via mouth-to-ear resuscitation, while on the child's little mind is printed, indelibly, Pork chops: terrible for dogs. Or maybe not. Chances are good he wasn't listening.

However, it's no wonder that the teacher doesn't want Junior's parents to help him with his homework. Junior has trouble enough keeping his grades up anyway. He doesn't need a headful of another generation's misinformation.

Each generation to its own misinformation, that's the way I look at it.

So there we are, all us parents, full of answers to questions that never get asked, standing around like cows at milking time the day the hired man left. And perhaps it's just as well.

It's not only that we did things differently then. I mean, way back when you took 3 from 0 and carried the 1. (I had never heard of number sets then, and I only wish my luck had held.) I mean, way back when you learned penmanship by something called the Palmer Method, which involved the whole arm from shoulder to fingertips, and the whole desk top. "Roll around-round-round-round-round," the teacher chanted, which made transparent sewer pipes if you did it right—

but I never could do it right. Or she'd go, "Push-pull-push-pull-push-pull."

(I know it sounds idiotic, children. That's because it was idiotic.)

But it isn't just the way we did things that was different. It's that we learned different facts, too.

For instance, I'm almost positive there were five instincts once. Eating. Propagating. Catching yourself if somebody dropped you. And two others I forget. (No aggressive instinct, though. We were all assumed to be naturally noble boys and girls, back in the public schools of Clayton, Missouri, and anyway we had the League of Nations.)

But then they lost an instinct somewhere, and then another one. Then it went up again in high school and down again in college and then I switched to English Lit. They never changed Milton. Should have, but didn't.

Yes, and once upon a time, way back when one Tootsie

Roll held you through the double feature and the serial and the Pathé News, there were twenty-four matched pairs of chromosomes. Then Science dropped one of *them.* And whatever happened to the Piltdown man? Who lost him? (Let's not always see the same hands.) And I can remember when the periodic table looked like a moth-eaten crib blanket. They've plugged up the holes now, I understand, but I don't know with what.

And back then, the atom was the littlest thing. And blue and green didn't go together. And Rosa Bonheur was a great painter. And Elizabeth Barrett Browning was a great romantic lady (now they tell me she was a hophead, I mean *hooked!*). And Freud was doing fine. And so were Latvia and Estonia, though I never could tell them apart, because they were both just small, pink places on the Europe map, but then they got pinker and disappeared altogether. And Stalin was a Good Guy. And so on. And so on.

Thus, the middle-aged brain, like a nicely marbled roast, seems to be shot through with facts that aren't so. And with so many of them, it's as though we had read the first newspaper story, SOCIALITE SHOOTS WIFE, but not the retraction, SOCIALITE NEVER SHOT WIFE AT ALL. Retractions seldom make the splash the original items did. And when they do, that's the day you didn't see the paper.

Anyway, it's easier to be dumb today, if that's any comfort, because there are so many more things to be dumb about. (You couldn't possibly be dumb about cryonics or ethology back when there weren't any, could you?) And in the last little while, if you looked away for an instant—and with a great many parents it's been a long instant—the landscape's all changed.[1]

"He said science was going to discover the basic secret of life some day," the bartender put in. He scratched his head and

frowned. "Didn't I read in the paper the other day where they'd finally found out what it was?"
"I missed that," I murmured.
"I saw that," said Sandra. "About two days ago."
"What *is* the secret of life?" I asked.
"I forget," said Sandra.

—KURT VONNEGUT, JR.

So it isn't surprising that many children consider their parents to be a little dim, and that they sometimes try to update them. The fact that they don't usually try too hard is just as well; a thoroughly updated parent is an unappetizing sight.

Nor is it surprising that the two generations often find the conversational going rough. As a result of time and television (there's real distance between *The Wind in the Willows* and Uncle Pookie), the allusive backgrounds are different.

Item: A neighbor of ours was explaining that his man Friday would run the office while the family was on vacation, and his nine-year-old son asked, "What's a man Friday?" When his father explained, the little boy nodded, knowledgeably. "Second banana," he murmured.

Item: I was trying to describe someone. "A Rhett Butler type," I said.

"Who's he?" asked our twelve-year-old.

"I mean he's a Clark Gable type," I amended quickly.

"Who's——"

"That's the hero in *Gone With the Wind*," explained our eighteen-year-old. She had seen the rerun.

"No, it's not," I said. "Rhett Butler was the hero."

"Not in the movie *I* saw," she said.

These things can be a little upsetting, at least to the senior generation.

"Actually, the whole business is rotten and unfair," says

Scott Corbett. "If some newcomer to puberty mentions the Rolling Stones in our presence and we respond with a blank expression, he looks down his pimply nose at us." And Mr. Corbett points out, further, that if we mention some really memorable name, the toast of six continents, whom Junior never heard of because Junior unluckily tuned in late, we still get the same pained look.

Clearly, then, for satisfying conversation, it is best to stick with one's peer group.

The other evening, my husband and I were having an intellectual discussion that reached an impasse when neither of us could remember who was responsible for "Poo poo dittem dottem whattem Chu." In fact, we reached the impasse and an argument simultaneously, for we couldn't agree on whether it was "Poo poo dittem dottem" or "*Boom boom* dittem dottem," which is the way we did it at my college. But he was hanging tough for Poo poo. Goodness only knows what college *he* went to.

However, the main question, to which we finally reverted, was: Who put it on the map?

Our twelve-year-old was listening.

"Edward Lear?" she hazarded, a little shyly. They had apparently reached Mr. Lear finally in their seventh-grade English.

"Shakespeare?" asked our eighteen-year-old from the window seat, where she was applying heart-shaped decals to her toenails.

And at that precise moment, my husband got that unlovable look on his face that indicates he knows something nobody else knows.

"I've got it," he said.

"I doubt it," I said.

"Ish Kabibble," he said.

"God bless you," said the eighteen-year-old.

"G'wan," I said to him, "yer mother wears army shoes."

"What was that again?" said the twelve-year-old, sometimes known as Ten-Watt.

But now I was remembering. It was coming back. For once he was right. Ish Kabibble. Kay Kyser. That May night in Ohio.

"Reet!" I cried. "I remember! At the spring formal—"

"What's a spring formal?" asked Twelve, sometimes known as Unawakened.

"It's a bash," explained her sister, sometimes known as Omniscient.

"Oh," said Twelve. "But who was Ish—"

"He was a fellow sang with Kay Kyser," I said, with impatience. "But listen—" (this to my husband)—"was that before the three little fitty or after?"

"Little what?" said Eighteen.

" 'Fitty and a mama fitty, too,' " I explained.

My husband passed me a pitying look. "It's the same song, remember? 'And dey fam and dey fam all over de dam. Poo poo—' "

" 'Boom boom,' " I said automatically.

"Cool it, Ma," murmured the eighteen-year-old, closing her eyes.

"Puke City," contributed Twelve, ever valiant.

But I am tenacious, if little else. "If you're so smart," I said to my husband, "who did——"

"And in case you're wondering," he rolled right over me, " 'Poo poo dittem dottem' came at least two years before 'Hut sut rawsun on the rilla-ra.' "

" 'And the brawla brawla'— It *did?*" I said, impressed in spite of myself. "You're right! And what about 'bo bope ska deeten dotten wotten dotten ch?' "

Eighteen looked at Twelve. "Would you *believe?*" she said.

"Awaaay we go," said Twelve.

And she was right; they couldn't stop me now.

" 'Bo bope ska deeten dotten wotten dotten ch!' " I said clearly. " 'Itch biddely otten dotten bo bope ska deeten dotten, itten bitten wittel little, bo bope ska deeten dotten wotten dotten ch.' "

Eighteen gathered her decals and her toes together and stood up. "Come on," she said. "Let's go watch Four Stiffs & a Live One."

"They on tonight?" said her sister. "Tough!"

"What?" I said.

"She means, What good news, she's delighted to hear it," Eighteen translated, painstakingly. "Come on." She beckoned, and the two headed for the stairs, each with her long hair flopping over one eye. "N.O.C.H.," she added, to her little sister.

"What?" said Twelve.

"Not Our Class, Honey," I heard her explain, comfortingly.

"And listen, you two!" I bawled after them. "Why don't you do something about those Veronica Lake hairdos. They went out with the Big Apple."

NOTES

1. "The postgraduate student with a teaching fellowship has as much trouble understanding undergraduates who are only four or five years younger as an aged professor might have: sometimes even more. For a generation is now about five years."

—EARL WARREN

QUESTIONS & TOPICS FOR DISCUSSION WITH PEERS

1. Which looks funnier, the Scrod or the Jitterbug?
2. Which sounds funnier, Johnny Ray or Tiny Tim?
3. Which tastes worse, Bingburgers or Bubba-Burgers?
4. Does middle age know where it's going?
5. What do mamas and papas expect out of life, and will they ever get it with the kids hanging around?
6. Anyway, we know more about some things than the kids do, don't we?
7. Anyway, we've got more money than the kids do. Haven't we?
8. Why do they call the medulla oblongata the brain stem now? Or is that something else? Why don't they make up their minds?
9. Is DNA as good as Platformate? Explain.

PART THREE

Moot Points

"I don't necessarily agree with everything I say."

—MARSHALL MC LUHAN

CHAPTER NINE

*

Keep Warm, Take Plenty of Liquids . . .

BED IS A GOOD PLACE TO BE, MORE OFTEN than one customarily is. I think it should be more celebrated than it is. Much credit is given to the anonymous inventor of the wheel. But what of the anonymous inventor of the bed? It has given more pleasure to more people than the wheel, or even Apollo 8, 9, or 10, and on the whole it has caused less trouble.

Bed is a place to fall back and regroup. Going to sleep is purely delightful, or should be. Whatever the matter is, you're leaving it for a while, to its own devices. I know a man who finds going to sleep such a rewarding occupation that he does it twice a night; sets his alarm clock for 2:00 A.M., so he can be jolted awake with the pleasant knowledge that he needn't do anything about it except go back to sleep again.

It should be a big bed, with a shelf behind it or beside it, or at least a small table with a drawer in it for hiding chocolate bars and Ipse Dixit wrinkle remover. (Ipse Dixit went into the business a couple of years ago and made a pile.)

It should have large feather pillows on it. Down pillows are all right, too. If you like electric blankets, it should have one. If you prefer the warm weight of bedclothes, it should have that. No point having anything or anyone in bed you don't like.

Satin pillowcases are good, and amazingly cheap for how smooth they are. They don't exactly keep your coiffure pristine, as the ads insist, but they stay fairly pristine themselves, which is something. Satin sheets are probably good, too, but I never tried them. Or you can make handsome sheets yourself, ʘʘ quite easily, in your choice of fetching patterns in smooth wide cotton, being sure to make a horizontal seam, not vertical. Then take your old sheets and cut them up for dust covers; you want to keep your dust looking nice.

That's about all you need. Don't furnish it too thoroughly or you'll have to housekeep it too much. Comfort is the word; not too stunning or you'll feel out of place. Still, not too ugly either. An attractive carafe or vacuum bottle is handy, especially if you run a self-service establishment. Once, when I was ailing, I had a vacuum jug in camel-dung brown with a red bellyband, homeliest thing you ever saw. I never really started to improve till I began pouring my coffee or bourbon-and-soda out of another one, made of dull spun-aluminum, much better looking.

Then some books behind the bed and some magazines under it (I find that when they're on it they slide off it). But each to his own decor.

More people should stay in bed more often than they do. While I frequently wish that I had never gotten out of bed that day, even more frequently I wish that certain other people hadn't. Therefore, if you ever feel like staying in bed all day but feel obscurely that you shouldn't, think of the trouble it might save somebody if you did, and do it.

From bed, things look faraway and unimportant, as a great many of them are. Staying in bed also rests your heart and your feet.

There you are, in bed. "And at the dead-center sits, motionless and spider-like, the uncanny soul." I don't think Logan Pearsall Smith was talking about bed when he said that. But it is a good line that I almost didn't remember in time to put in. In bed, thoughts are sometimes fuzzy and hard to grab, like the cotton in the aspirin bottle.

Now, being sick has given bed a bad name. Someone tells you he was in bed all last week, by himself, and you think, What a shame, instead of, How nice.

In fact, being sick has given being sick a bad name. OO There is nothing the matter with being sick that getting well can't fix, unless you are sick on a gorgeous, fragrant spring day. There you are, nongorgeous, nonfragrant, and feeling like a dropout to boot, which can spoil the whole thing. You should be sick on a raw, rotten day. Then you can lie there feeling raw, rotten, and obscurely cozy.

You want to be sick from the neck down, never from the neck up. This eliminates toothaches, migraine, earaches, eyeaches, hang-overs, facial neuralgia, sinus trouble, and the common cold, all snuffly and rasp-throated and germy.

Better be abed with a broken leg than plain old-fashioned hoarse and buggy.

ʘʘ Then, sprained ankles are good, and so are pulled muscles of all sorts, and simple fractures. I had a mild neuritis once that I rather enjoyed. There are probably many other good things, too, that I haven't had yet. (Another good thing is a general admonition from the doctor to take it easy, unless it scared you right into a decline.)

Then there is the matter of pain. I mean pasteurized pain—only a tablespoon's worth in the world's cupful, but still the only kind most of us know in our lucky little segment of time and space. Not premeditated or inflicted pain, psychotically enjoyed by the inflicter, and accompanied by fright and despair. I mean pain that just comes along, which well-disposed and knowledgeable people try to ameliorate or banish, though they can't always.

Modern children are not aware of this, in the easy, protected parts of our hemisphere. There is a shot or a deadener for everything, or so they think. Accordingly, they are usually in for some rude shocks.

It is too bad they can't grow up better oriented; can't be given a flash of several kinds of pain, so they would understand how Grandpa was feeling, that day at the zoo when he bit the tiger and then wouldn't pop for the popcorn. But it's hard to think of any kindly way to do this.

Also, they should learn a little earlier than they do (and, of course, some buoyant glowing people never learn it, though I'm not sure they are entirely fortunate) that the mental climate of the sick is another climate, rather like that of the person who has had one drink more than he needs. Emphases are different, not to say unusual. This can explain a lot.

Indeed, pain discolors time, like a red sock in the wash

water. It bleeds into what it touches. But it certainly passes the time, and is, in its own way, interesting—that is, until it becomes so bad that you can't observe it objectively any longer, can only swing with it.

Otherwise, it can be an absorbing hobby. Either it sits in the corner like a monstrous mother-in-law, fouling the atmosphere, or it's all over you; but either way it demands total involvement, like championship bridge. (Most pain is more totally involving than most pleasure.) And in your innocent self-absorption you can tend your pain like a garden, and time goes more rapidly than it does, for instance, when you are traveling.

Indeed, pain is another country—the country of Little-Ease?—with its own customs and imperatives. Even a bad head cold is an island connected to the mainland by a perilously frail causeway.

And it can give rise to monologues of dazzling dullness: "Let's see, I took a pain pill at 2:00 A.M., but then I took a capsule at three, and if I took a sleeping pill *now* . . ." and so on. But it is of acute interest to the pain feeler.

A problem is this: pain, like gusto, is not communicable. It is not even believable, when it is someone else's. Not *really* believable. That is why it is dull to hear about after the first time around, like a detailed travelogue of someone's trip through the Lesser Deltoids, a place the listener hasn't been to and doesn't intend to visit.

And so you concentrate on your pain, and move warily around it, if you move at all. Then, if it starts to recede, you prod it furtively, as you'd poke a snake with a stick to see if it still wiggles.

It is interesting, when you hurt, to ask yourself, How much *are* you hurting? How hot would you register on the painometer? Is this pain really this big, or are you inventing some of it? Any confirmation that it *is* this big is, of course, to be welcomed. Good painside manners, when someone else is suffering, demand that you say, "I had that once and it's the worst thing I ever had in my whole life." You are his true friend.

Harold Wolff, a pain researcher, said, "We early discovered, much to our surprise, that all human beings have the same threshold; the point at which they first perceive pain is the same for all persons."

Therefore, the difference must be in one's promptness in saying Ouch. And in whether or not one says it aloud. And how loud.

I generally find myself pulled in two directions. I want the credit for behaving admirably under difficult circumstances. But how will people know the circumstances are difficult unless I tell them so?

Like the pleasure of doing a good deed in private and having it discovered in public, it is delightful when someone accidentally discovers how atrocious you are feeling and how good you are being. But this can't always be arranged.

It is customary to think that one would prefer, on the whole, living with a large physical pain to living with a large psychic pain. This is one of those things that not many people get to prove, which probably saves a lot of face. (Like, would you rather marry a terribly rich man you didn't love or a terribly poor man you love? It is customary to say you'd opt for the poor man, but girls don't always do that when they get a chance to opt.)

I don't know. I doubt if anyone knows, till he's visited awhile in both places.

Among the worst pains I know is knowing the only thing that can assuage it is whatever or whoever gave it to you in the first place: the aching heart (because of your lover) or the aching tooth (because of your dentist, for it hadn't given you a speck of trouble till he filled it) or the aching spirit (because of a job you cannot do but must do).

Pains like this are the more exquisite because you know that with your own little two feet you must track down their originators, and, when you get there, they will very likely hand you some more.

Another hard thing to endure is not knowing how long you must endure. Pain should come packaged, like refrigerated ready-to-bake yeast bread, bearing the date when it becomes inoperative. But you still have the fifth freedom, of attitude. They cannot change that.

A clean pain has it all over a mussy pain. Pain is enough by itself, without festering. Or being ridiculous. I certainly want some dignity in my pain, but that is hard to come by. For instance, at the dentist's (see your dentist twice a chapter), you look simply dim-witted, your open mouth stuffed full of machinery that prevents your asking intelligent questions, like What do you think you're trying to do?

And there's no dignity to giving birth. There you are in approximately the same position that got you into this fix, only more muss, and there's no dignity to being born either, bare-bottomed and head first; and both of these are reasonably painful procedures. But neither is there much grace left to dying, now they have you plumbed like an *espresso* machine or carved up like a Christmas goose the third helping around. Perhaps it's as well that we get a chance to practice on the other indignities so we are better prepared to star in the final performance.

Pain isn't ennobling while you're having it, necessarily. During the fifteen years Karl Marx worked on *Das Kapital*, he suffered from an enlarged liver, hemorrhoids, recurrent eye infections, insomnia, and boils. Once they heard him muttering that "the bourgeoisie would have cause to remember my carbuncles." Indeed, indeed . . .

And yet, pain can make you awfully sweet when it quits, which is one of the good reasons for having some. Nonpain is perilously close to heaven, after a rousing bout of it—a fact known to many, and cogently expressed by some.

Isak Dinesen includes it in her three kinds of perfect happiness: "(1) to feel in one's self an excess of strength (2) to have been in pain and to have it cease (3) to know for certain that you are fulfilling the will of God."

Jessamyn West writes persuasively of the glory that precedes her bouts with migraine, and of the bliss that follows them: "As the pain lets up, my world extends an inch, a foot, a yard beyond my brow. And in so small a world I see things I never saw before. I don't ever remember seeing a shoe before, seeing it, that is, as other than something created whole, the offspring of another shoe, an object as integral as an egg. As the pain retreated and the world outside the skull came into focus I saw one of my red loafers beside the bed. It was as pretty as a daisy to me, but much stranger. I picked it up and turned it over and about in my hand, filled with a kind of cheerful marveling content. . . ."

And the theologian William Paley says that pain is "seldom both violent and long-continued; and its pauses and intermissions become positive pleasures. It has the power of shedding a satisfaction over intervals of ease, which few enjoyments exceed."

And so pain has its positive virtues, which is a good thing, inasmuch as it is hard to avoid. Simply feeling poorly has its advantages, moreover, because when you feel too good, you don't want to waste that exuberance on something conscientious or constructive.

Indeed, a sudden rush of health can be as disconcerting as a sudden pain. Before I stopped smoking the first time,

I had been warned that I would experience moments of feeling funny. This wasn't necessarily nerves, the expert said, it was all those little red blood cells standing erect, breathing deep, and flexing their biceps. It happened, too, and believe me, I wouldn't want to go through that again. Didn't do a lick of work for weeks.

It has been said, and I imagine with truth, that two thirds of the world's work is done by people who aren't feeling very good. A lot of it looks like it, too. Still, when you think of the snuffles, cramps, fantods, and general malaise of the spirit that probably went into your new suit, it's no wonder the buttons keep coming off. If it hadn't been for all those ailments, the suit would likely never have got made at all.

Sometimes I lie here and think about these things.

QUESTIONS & TOPICS FOR DISCUSSION WITH OTHER WOMEN

(*Men don't like discussions like this*)

1. How many stitches did you have?

2. Would you rather have a big pain that shows, like a busted head, or a big pain that doesn't show, like a slipped disc?

Really?

3. If a vitamin pill supplies vitamins, does a pain pill . . .

Oh, well . . .

4. Wouldn't it be awful to have poison oak under your cast? I knew a man who did. Nearly lost his mind, too.

CHAPTER TEN

Wet Birds

ONE DAY I RECEIVED A LETTER FROM A LITTLE magazine asking me what was the best advice I ever received. They were asking a great many people, in order to do an article about it.

I didn't have anything on tap, and I wondered at the time if the other interviewees did. Articles like that never seem to me quite believable. Like the "My Favorite Recipe" collections, to which I've been asked to contribute. I find that wishful thinking keeps getting into them, at least with me. I always tend to pick a recipe that I wish I were the kind of person this would be the favorite recipe of, if you follow me. . . .

So I thought up some advice to send the magazine, and though I can't remember what it was, I do remember reflecting that the best advice I ever received is probably the advice I forgot the minute I heard it—forgot it out of self-defense, probably, because the best advice usually sounds like work, or in one way or another pretty grim.

It's a shame. Good advice is a fine thing, and there's a lot of it going around now. But I've noticed that I always catch the little ones while the big ones swim away.

Why don't the little ones swim away, too? Or fly? But no, they stay put, like Jackie Vernon's wet birds. His grandfather, on his deathbed, whispered in Jackie's ear, "Remember, boy, wet birds don't fly at night." Jackie remembered, all right; can't forget it, as a matter of fact; suspects there's a real depth charge hidden somewhere in his grandpa's last words. But it continues to elude him.

It is comforting to know that other people have the same trouble. Take the case of a girl I know. Her uncle once told her that she'd always better pry the cork out of the soft-drink bottle caps, because there's one company—he forgot which one—that puts stars in some, which they will redeem for $100. My friend can't forget it; and whenever she is missing from the group at a party, you'll find her out in the kitchen, rather hopelessly reaming out cap after cap. . . .

Then, somebody told me once that you shouldn't say anything unless it met the three specifications of being a) kind, b) true, and c) necessary. For years I was tongue-tied; couldn't think of a thing that fitted all three, except for something like "Ahoy there, you nice person, I'm drowning, and if it isn't too much trouble would you save me?" Situations like that never came up.

Another thing I've noticed about advice is that one seldom remembers the polished profundities that someone clears his throat before uttering. What sticks is the random thought dropped casually, more or less unnoticed by the dropper. I mean the words—as Mark Twain put it—that stew out of somebody naturally, like the precious otter of roses out of the otter.

"You haven't finished the dishes till you've scrubbed the sink," my mother once remarked. ("I *did?*" she said, when I quoted it back, years later.) I'm sure she delivered many more rarefied bits, but that is the one that stuck. I don't know why, unless for the same reason or lack of it that a friend of mine remembers exclusively her mother's dictum, "Never check a laundry list; the price of a washrag isn't worth it." *

Another friend of mine remembers only the worried maternal admonition, "If you must be a wallflower, dear, don't take root, move around a little."

It made me wonder what pearls I might have strewn along the way. So I asked my daughter. She couldn't think of any, immediately, but she brought the subject up again the next night.

"I remember!" she said. "You told me once, 'Never stare at the sun.' "

"I *did?*" I said. I had hoped for something a little more—well—significant?

Clearly, the mother-daughter relationship is pre-eminently practical.

Then I've wondered about advice from teachers. What do you carry away besides a diploma? Surely some sound educational sediment is deposited. But what about shiny nuggets?

I remember few, myself, all tiny. I remember a grade-school teacher who always added an extra *i* to words, like mischievious and mountainious, though she made up for it

* This was before king-size sheets.

by taking the *i* out of words like alluval, and who stressed Originality, as we have just seen. "Be Original," she wrote in a firm clear hand on the blackboard. And one day, to prove her point, she cited the title of her college valedictory thesis, "Out of School Life, Into Life School," which I remember thinking was *terribly* good. But that is all I do remember. . . . Besides a high-school professor who told us, with a baleful eye, "Never say enthuse." I never have.

My friend Marion (I did some research on this) says she can still see, in her mind's eye, a college professor with a prominent Adam's apple and bright blue eyes, leaning across the podium in mortal exasperation, yelling, "Look, I'm offering you a dollar and you're only taking fifty cents!" My friend admits ruefully that she herself hadn't taken a nickel, because she can't remember what the course was.

And a man I know remembers his art teacher saying, "Don't forget now, the blackest blacks come next to the whitest whites." It struck my friend as sort of philosophical.

Well, then—fathers? Fathers tend to pontificate a bit, and surely . . .

"Do you remember any advice of your father's?" was my question.

"I certainly do," said my friend Patricia, promptly. "He said, 'Be careful what you name a horse.' " (It seems that her father, who had owned and loved many horses, had learned that they generally live up to their names. His Firesweep was a whirlwind, and Peacetime was a contemplative, and one colt, named Largely, grew up to be seventeen hands high. Finally he acquired a colt by Upset, the only horse to beat Man o' War, and tried to teach him to jump. The colt's name was Bang Crash, and that is precisely what he did.)

A man I know enjoyed many a long talk with his father, who was a world traveler, a construction engineer, and a

Federal judge. My friend's sole paternal talisman is "Always whittle away from yourself."

I have tried hard to think what words I have from my own father, who was an educator and a thoughtful man. Finally I remembered. "Don't run with your hands in your pockets." I consider this to be, at any rate, more practical than the other two, for one does more running in this world than whittling or naming horses, or so I have found, though all three are a far cry from Polonius. Still, look what happened to Polonius.

CHAPTER ELEVEN

*

If You'll Promise Not to Tell Me about Your Trip, I Promise Not to Tell You about Mine

I KNOW THAT TRAVEL IS BOTH ENRICHING AND impoverishing, in about equal proportions, though the enrichment probably has the edge. Still, I've never found conversations about it to be particularly rewarding, no matter which end of them I'm on.

Perhaps you are intimately acquainted with the habitat and migratory pattern of the Number 11 bus, or with the only pub in Whitehall shaped like a bottle. But what can I say when you report this, except "Is that a fact!"

And if I describe in rare detail how I finally learned to

operate the grate in my Edinburgh bed-sitter just before I was totally gassed, how can I expect you to be glad of it.

And so one generally trots out merely the tin—the funny bartender, the firkins and kilderkins of Guinness—and hugs the gold. (How goes it with the head of Blessed Oliver Plunket now, and the wild swans at Coole?) And if you're not careful, the trip can lose a bit of its shimmer, fast as the bloom goes out of the stateside muumuu.

It is bad enough, of course, talking to someone who's never crossed a county line. How explain the feel of the Old Town, the slant of the sun on baroque roofs, the gray taste of Czech bread? Or the warmed-honey feel of the waters around Kauai? The best snapshots are only shiny paper, and the best slides lack the fourth, or personal, dimension.

But even worse is talking to someone who has, indeed, been where you've been. There is a lady I meet frequently—ran into her only yesterday, as a matter of nonfact—and she greeted me with enthusiasm.

"Welcome home!" she cried. "I understand you've been to my favorite city!"

"Which one would that be?" I asked, cautiously.

"Vienna!" she said. "Heavenly Wien!"

"Why, yes, I certainly have!" I beamed, and I settled down happily for a chat.

"What did you think of the Holdrichsmühle?" she asked.

"The what?"

"The Holdrichsmühle. And Heiligenkreuze. And the Babenbergers!"

"I'm afraid I didn't try a Babenberger," I said. "That is, we were eating so much anyway, you know how it goes, the Sacher *torte* and the *Schlagobers*. . . ." In fact, I've wondered, now we have Dramamine, why they don't invent a pill that keeps you hungry. Because otherwise . . .

"You don't eat Babenbergers; they're buried there," she said. "You know—old Frederick the Bellicose and all."

"No, I didn't know," I said. But that reminded me of the Hapsburg crypts. Twenty tons of pewter just to hold down Marie Therese! Or maybe that was in the Heiligenkreuze? But I wasn't about to ask my little friend. So I said, "But I did see—"

"The Lippizaner horses? They're my pets!"

"No, they were on vacation or something," I said. "But I saw the—"

"Storks?" she said.

"What storks?" I said.

"Oh, come *on!* That place! The place where the storks roost!"

"No, I'm afraid I didn't," I said. But that made me think of the Danish Riviera, where I had been visiting, too, and the salt-water swans swooping around. You should get as many points for a salt-water swan as you do for a roosting stork, it seems to me. . . .

"Speaking of storks," I said, "I was amazed at the—"

"Bargains? You *did* do some shopping, didn't you?"

"Yes, I did," I said. "I got to the—"

"To the wrought-iron place? Where they do the marvelous garden stuff?"

"No, I didn't know about that," I said. "But I bought some awfully pretty petit—"

"I hope you didn't buy any of the petit point," she said. "It's such a cliché. But you *did* find that divine little studio where they copy the excavated jewelry?"

"No," I said.

But I did too see Vienna. And I'm very fond of my petit-point handbag.

Maybe it's a matter of wave length, this travel talk, and there are many wave lengths.

Take Mother, who returned not long ago from Europe, with a short hang-over in the British Isles on the way home. She and I were about to have some coffee the other day in her kitchen. Mother prefers drip coffee, black, hot, strong, and fresh, the water added one tablespoonful at a time, which always takes a good while.

"I just don't know," she said. "They're going to have to *do* something about the situation over there," and I noticed to my surprise that the hand that rocked the coffeepot was shaking a little.

I've always liked the Keep Calm sign on the French planes, *Ne Perdez Pas Votre Sang Froid.* Was mother losing hers?

"What do you mean?" I asked.

"It's simply too uncomfortable, all over," she said. "France, Scotland, Ireland, Yugoslavia . . ."

Uncomfortable. It was a new thought to me. Although perhaps (I thought) I've tended to overestimate the comfort over there because of the magnificent contrast with what probably went before. Sitting Down, after doing the Vatican. Or getting warm, finally, on a winter Sunday in Wales, where Sunday starts early and lasts several years. Indeed, the most voluptuously comfortable moments of my life, I spent by a brass-bright fire, snug and safe from the razor-edged sleet the color of coal dust, in Llanfairpwllgwyngyllgogerychwyrndrobwllllantysiliogogogoch. . . . But I didn't feel up to name-dropping.

"They've got to do something," Mother said again.

"Like what?" I said. I've always found it best to humor Mother.

"Because if they don't," she said, disregarding my question (Mother often disregards my questions), "we'll all do what we probably ought to do anyway, stay right here at home and save our money. And our feet. Those cobblestones!" she said. "I noticed, in Tivoli, I kept hunting for the softer cobblestones. But there weren't any. And every morning I'd lie there in bed, making bets with myself which pair of shoes I'd be able to put on. If any."

"Mother, I *told* you to take some old tennis shoes along," I said. "You can always pry your feet into old tennis shoes. And anyway they're picturesque."

"The tennis shoes?" she asked.

"The cobblestones," I said.

"But you can't walk on them," she said, with finality. "Not a reason in the world they can't have decent paved sidewalks like we do. Or *moving* sidewalks, that's the ticket. Up and down the streets and around the ruins."

"But then you couldn't stand and stare," I said. "Whoosh, there went the Acropolis. Zoom, there went the Schönbrunn. . . . You know, Mother, I remember just standing and staring in the Grosse Galerie and I thought I could hear little Mozart playing!"

"Must have been your imagination," said Mother briskly. "Coffee?" And she poured some.

"Yes, thank you," I said.

"But all the same—" I began again.

"And the bathroom paper!" Mother said. "There's a place for waxed paper, but the bathroom isn't it."

"Yes, I know," I said, remembering. And yet, I always felt that the other bathroom amenities one runs into make up for a great deal. Grandma Cuddlefinger running the rest room under Piccadilly, with her teapot and her knitting and her sharp eye on the customers. And the heated towel rods other places, and the lovely bidets . . .

"And the butter," said Mother.

"Butter?" I echoed.

"I never saw butter in Dubrovnik," Mother said. "And the coffee—unspeakable!" (As I have indicated, Mother likes her coffee.) "You chew it," she said, "then pick it out of your teeth all day."

"Yes, but—" I wanted to tell her about breakfast in the village outside Prague where breakfast was coffee and salami, with a spray of blueberries surrounding a stack of tiny poppy-seed rolls; and the little old black-aproned lady who'd picked the blueberries, having coffee with us, carefully spooning the sediment out of her cup, licking her toothless chops at every bite. I mean, *chacun à son café,* I always say, but Mother was rushing on.

"And the bedding!" she said. "Those slip-covered quilts!"

"But they're so pretty," I said. "And practical, too."

"Practically useless," she snorted. "Pull 'em up and you roast, down and you freeze."

Well . . .

"Wasn't London an improvement?" I asked.

"London?" She rolled her eyes. "Honestly! It's so Americanized you wouldn't believe it. Modern? You can't see the chimney pots for the TV antennas. All *over* Britain."

"I know," I admitted, uneasily. I was aware that it's not all Dickens and ale and Paddy's pig. I remembered my dismay a few years ago, seeing the L'il Abner movie at Tregenna Castle. But, on the other hand, I remembered London in 1950, and an ad on a movie screen, "Forsooth, 'tis Lady Ruth! Knitted sweaters for ladies." Carnaby Street has changed that, and it can't help but be for the better.

"Well—" I said to Mother. "Isn't Americanizing what you wanted?"

Mother glared at me. "A Betta-Burger quick lunch just down from The Cheshire Cheese? That sky line, like Chicago? And people talking the same language?"

"Oh, but they don't," I said. "They're so much politer."

And I mentioned the London chemist who kept saying Kyo.

"What's Kyo?" said Mother.

"Thank you," I said. "But they bury it in their tonsils so it comes out Kyo, didn't you notice? Six Kyos for one transaction! I asked for nail polish and he said 'Kyo, what kind, mum?' And I told him and he said Kyo, and then he handed it to me and said Kyo, and—"

"Sounds dim-witted," Mother said. "And I'll bet it was American nail polish, wasn't it?"

"Well, yes," I said, remembering my pleasure at finding my favorite shade. "Anyway, I'll bet the English toast is still cold," I comforted her.

"Well, yes," she said grudgingly. "Naturally. But the butter—"

"What about it?"

"Plenty of it," she said crossly. "Just like here."

"And decent sidewalks?"

"All over the place."

"Bedding?"

"Just like ours," she said bitterly. "Sheets, blankets—even electrics, some places—you'd never know you'd left home. They've just got to do something, that's all there is to it."

So I drank some more of Mother's good coffee, trying to think what.

QUESTIONS & TOPICS FOR DISCUSSION

1. "Fashions in landscapes change like any others, and to-day the hideous part of an otherwise beautiful country is the one to be sought: bone-bare Mykonos, the bleak chic of Port' Ercole and Porto Santo Stefano on what is perhaps the only really plain strip of Italian coast."

—ELEANOR PERENYI, *Vogue*

Explain.

2. Is it still okay to enjoy looking at the Matterhorn or the Taj Mahal so long as you don't tell anybody? Discuss.

3. Why doesn't *ananas* on a French menu mean bananas? Check French Academy.

4. Why do the English confuse their Publics with their Privates, with their Public Bar meaning Private Bar and Public School meaning Private School and so on?

5. Why does first floor always mean second floor on the Continent?

Why is the ladies' room always on it?

6. Why is it called The Continent when there are six others?

7. Why does a salt ocean leave you sticky?

8. How high can a bird fly on Tuesday?

CHAPTER TWELVE

Of Books and Bookkeeping

"I do retire
Into an old room, beside a bright fire."
—EDWARD FITZGERALD

THIS CHAPTER OF THIS BOOK IS ABOUT BOOKS, as astute readers will perceive, but not exactly about the enjoyment of books.

I have noticed that people who like books tend to brag about it, the way people brag about taking cold showers (different people, by the way; the two predilections seldom go together). And, often, they seem to assume that nobody else likes books, or really and truly deep-down appreciates them. Once I saw a book called *Reading Can Be Fun!*, a title that had a nice earnest idiocy, I thought, like *How to Enjoy a Good Laugh*.

Indeed, Constant Reader tends to get pretty smug. A bookish gentleman named Falkland concluded a paean to books with "I do pity unlearned gentlemen on a rainy day" —which statement implies, for one thing, that unbookish gentlemen are unlearned—a questionable assumption— and also commits the common error of supposing that because someone isn't having fun your way, he isn't having fun. Indeed, there are many other good and possibly more constructive activities for rainy days. Taking pictures, or walks, or time to stare. Or making anything from love to butterscotch brownies to music on the sitar . . .

And so, as I said, this chapter on books concerns itself mainly with other things about them.

I was surprised to find it a stubborn chapter to organize and write. The sentences kept separating and the paragraphs curdled. It was only when I was on the point of throwing it out that I discovered what the trouble was: I was trying to impose order on as disorderly a subject as anyone ever tackled sitting down. Books are legion, and of their making there is no end, nor of things to say about them.

Thus, you can imagine my relief when I happened upon the following words of John Ruskin's, in his prefatory note to his *Precious Thoughts* (1879):

> Much time is wasted by human beings, in general on establishment of systems; and it often takes more labor to master the intricacies of an artificial connexion, than to remember the separate facts which are so carefully connected. I purpose, therefore, henceforward to trouble myself little with sticks or twine, but to arrange my chapters with a view to convenient reference, rather than to any careful division of subjects, and to follow out, in any byways that may open, on right hand or left, whatever question it seems useful at any moment to settle.

Ruskin clearly understood how these things go, or don't

go. I didn't think he would mind my borrowing his apologia as well as his system, skipping the sticks and twine.

Accordingly, I have alphabetized my points as far as I could, using a somewhat modified Dewey decimal system. This did away with the need for neat transitions—a help right there—though it dropped me immediately right into the middle of a big problem area:

811:22
K
BOOKS, Arrangement of

There is no ideal arrangement of, though there are many approaches.

Some people solve it, or think they do, with an admirable directness. They put the best-looking books in the best-looking rooms and the rest somewhere else.

However, the reason they can be so neat about it all is that they don't read their books enough to disturb them—their good-looking books, anyway—and the fact becomes apparent if you visit these people occasionally. Like a fixed smile, every tooth in place, those books are always the same. And so it turns out that these people aren't telling you what they thought they were telling you about themselves. Then there is the conversation-piece approach, though I've had poor luck with it, myself. On occasion, before guests have arrived, I've arranged a few telling tidbits on the cocktail table—say, Mrozek's *Elephant* or *The Kama Sutra*. But no one ever noticed them, and they started no conversation, and I needn't have bothered.

You could arrange them in strict alphabetical order, by author, except that who can remember who wrote *The Diagnostics of Human Behavior* or *The Sportsman's Handbook*? Or by color, if that's the way you remember books. But the color usually changes when the jackets come off, and anyway the rest of the family may not be so color-minded.

Or by genre: fiction, verse, biography, and so forth. Still, in this day of the nonfiction novel and the fictionalized autobiography and the biographical verse drama, the lines are fuzzy.

I rather favor putting the dull ones together and the delightful ones together, like guests. But what do you do, then, about the stretch of stodge in the middle? (Speaking of dull, Katharine Whitehorn writes, "My grandfather's books inherited a classification with them. He was given to owning, and indeed writing, books with titles like *'God in the Slums'*; his irreverent children lumped them all together under the name of the dread disease, *'Slod in the Gums.'* ")

811:23
K
BOOKS, as Albums

Most people have some big books around that they never look at—*The Illustrated History of Glass-Blowing,* or *Our Heritage of This and That*—that is, books you get for Christmas from well-meaning friends who don't know you very well. It does little good to spread these around the living room, because all it proves is that you have some well-meaning friends who don't know you very well, and who doesn't?

The best thing to do with them is to make photograph albums out of them, assuming you take pictures. I mean snapshots, the old-fashioned Oops-I-cut-your-feet-off sort of pictures that tend to pile up so badly; I don't mean slides or movies.

Nearly always, one has more snapshots than albums. So what you do, without telling any sentimental book people I suggested it, is this: get one of those big nonbooks and paste the snapshots in, right over the type, on the first page. Then cut out the next two pages, as close to the left-hand side of the page as you can, and paste pictures on the next one. Cut out two more, and so on, so the book won't get unbearably swollen. You can take care of a lot of snapshots this way, and a lot of books, too, and their authors will never know.

811:24
K
BOOKS, Explicit

I've always favored the word *explicit* or *sexplicit* over *dirty,* because if sex books are called dirty, it is tacit that sex is. Indeed, it wonders me, those nervous parents who self-consciously try to tell their children that Sex Is Beautiful, then yell at them the next minute to stay away from those dirty books.

A librarian whose name I wish I knew, and whose letter I wish I had kept (it appeared in *Saturday Review*), proposed a solution to at least one part of the explicit-book problem. Speaking of how the gamier ones—*Lady Chatterley's Lover, Portnoy,* and so on—come back with the choicer pages virtually illegible from fingerprints, peanut butter, and steamy breathing, she said it was a great expense to the library, replacing the volumes. She recommended that one superbly complete and explicit book be issued—absolutely *everything* in it, dozens of copies to each library. In comparison, *Portnoy* would read like *Sunnybrook Farm,* and no one but people writing master's theses would take it out, and worth-while savings would be effected.

It is a practical approach; and I think, myself, that the book could well be government issue, one to a family. (Everything the government prints looks so dull that the children would never read it anyway.) I see it as a loose-leaf format, with sheets issued periodically, whenever new perversions, positions, fetishes, and so forth are discovered or invented. Or, possibly, when you've sent your income-tax check in. This could speed payments.

B101:J9
BOOKS, for the Flu

A proper home library needs a flu shelf, or a broken leg shelf. It's wise to pick these things up when you're healthy and put them away for when you're not. What you have on your flu shelf is, of course, your own business, for everyone has his tolerances. I found Camus's *The Plague* quite satisfactory once when I had an Asian virus, for I felt better by comparison. But when my fever went over 102°, I was missing too much, so I had to subside to somebody small and easy, I forget who. Never high-hat the small-and-easies, for they can best ameliorate small troubles (while great troubles can be helped only by great books, if they can be helped by any). Inasmuch as there are more little troubles than big ones, our literary balance is probably about right.

Logically, being sick should be a good time for rereading novels one always intended to reread; but, illogically, it seldom is. You're ailing anyway, and rereading most novels is like a drag on a dead cigarette.

811:25
K
BOOKS, Learning from, vs. Learning from Television

It is too easy to beat television over the rabbit ears, and while you're doing it, you'll miss the program on John Donne's sonnets, the panel on communications, the ecology seminar, and the Spanish lesson, all of which are on this morning, as I write.

That's one trouble: I work in the morning, and so when the TV feels like teaching, I don't feel like paying attention; and when I feel like learning something, they give me Don Rickles.

Then, the telly and I seldom agree on what to study, when. It is touring the Prado the night I want to read about the Romanovs. And on a foggy day when a picture tour would be just the ticket, they give me a kidney transplant. Books are more co-operative.

But worst of all is the handicap of being invincibly word-minded, as opposed to picture-minded. People who grow up seeing more pictures than they read words take naturally to television and apparently learn from it easily. It is what Marshall McLuhan calls the immediate impact as opposed to the linear, assuming I understand McLuhan, which is as major an assumption as you've made in some time.

But to me, the impact isn't immediate, it is diffused, *rayonné,* like a child's drawing of the sun—each straight line leading away from the meat of the matter.

Take a television scientist explaining nucleic acids. I notice that he doesn't pronounce "nucleic" quite the way I do. I resolve to look it up. Meanwhile, he's galloped ahead into five-carbon sugar molecules and I've missed the connection. This is annoying. I look at him afresh. He is a tall man with sandy hair and a thin mouth. My mother once told me (from what well of sour experience, I never knew) never to trust tall sandy-haired men with thin mouths. I wonder why. Who did what to Mom? Of course, there's a lot you'll never know about your own mother. . . .

There he stands, this scientist, now making molecule diagrams on a blackboard, only it looks more like football. The Green Bay Packers' zone defense. Nucleic acids, I believe, was the subject. What drove him to this?

. . . And so it goes. If the wool I gather during one short instructive program were packed into a mattress, I'd probably fall asleep on it even sooner than I do on the sofa.

Still, the picture-oriented have problems, too. I remember seeing the network anchor man at the last Republican convention catch himself in the act of checking the monitor set to see what the chairman was doing, when the chairman was only ten feet away. It is too bad if we become so accustomed to seeing through a cameraman's eyes that we can't use our own.

811:26
K
BOOKS, Lending

There is really no good way to lend books, or not to. When you lend a book, chances are excellent that you won't see it again. (People are usually punctilious about returning a $6.95 bottle of Scotch, but not a $6.95 book.) Still, refusing to lend a book makes for an awkward moment. Once, a man brought out his book-lending notebook and asked me to sign the book out. Obviously he didn't trust me, and with good reason. But I was furious, I can tell you.

A problem is that other people's books often seem more interesting than the people, especially at cocktail parties. (In fact, any television program would probably be more interesting than most cocktail conversation, though probably no more so than the Cocktail Acquaintance would be had he devoted a week's hard work to his preparation, as the TV show did.) Book-minded guests often wish the host would pour a drink all around and then let the people read. But I doubt if he ever will.

Weekend cottage books are attractive, too—that is, a cottage where you're visiting. Usually it is a strangely static literary lineup, the complete works of George Eliot, unravished, forever fair, only a bit mildewed, plus some vintage Chandler and Hammett. *And,* usually, something you've been wanting to read for years. Not that you'll get to, though. You'll probably have to go hike or swim or some damn thing.

811:27
K
BOOKS, Not Owning Any

This can be a real pleasure, especially if you've moved your household chattels several times recently; and depending on who did your moving, it may work out that way. No books to dust, or step over, or feel conscience-ridden about not having read. Just a library card. And some people wouldn't even miss the library card. "How many books do you think I'll need?" a young actress asked Dorothy Rodgers, who was going to decorate her apartment.

Still, if we can agree, tentatively, that reading books is a Good Thing, I suppose everyone should have a few. (Like the gun laws. If you have a gun in the house, chances are mathematically a little better that you'll pick it up some day and shoot somebody.)

I would miss books, myself, for many reasons, not the least of which is lying on the sofa when you don't feel like reading, and—as you look at the familiar bindings—tasting the books in your head, re-creating the era, the aura, the people, rather in the same way a musician reads a printed score and hears the music.

Oddly enough, unread books have their place in this picture, too. You can visualize or imagine not only what's in the book but also the frame of mind (vigorous, merry, contemplative, erotic) that you want to be in when you read it, which is rather fun, too.

811:28
K
BOOKS, Paperbacked

Paperbacks have dignity now. I know some people who tailored their bookshelves to paperback size, to house a good library that cost them less than $150.

Also, you can tear pages out of paperbacks, thus acquiring a nice clutch of the best parts, like packaged chicken thighs or breasts, no necks or gizzards. This takes up little space. Or use the same technique, in a crisis, for group reading. Driving home from a fishing trip once, through dreary country, all of us tired and talked out, the girl in front started a good thriller and passed it back, page by page, to me. It was a help.

Another thing—you can find plain jackets for paperbacks now, and if you can't find them, they're easy to make, out of bright rugged fabric. (It's good to include a handle so you can wear it on your wrist.)

These can be handy if you don't want people to see you reading *Necrophilia Can Be Fun,* as well as for other special circumstances. A friend of mine has an eleven-year-old who is a very meaty reader: Kant, Hegel, James, and the like. Whenever they travel, she insists that he keep his reading under wraps, else she couldn't take him anywhere for half fare.

811:29
K
BOOKS, Rapid Reading of

I don't think much of it, nor do I know many writers who do. The reason is probably selfish. As a woman is understandably undone when a large, laboriously prepared dinner gets eaten in ten minutes, so is a writer who sees someone read in an hour what it took him four years to write. It is illogical, but so.

B:101:J15

BOOKS, Underlining in

This is quite all right if it is your own book. My own family is rather given to doing this, as well as splattering the margins with vigorous comments, like *Birdseed!* or *Splendid!* or even (in books that have been in the family quite a while) *And how!*

Too, cookbooks that have been underlined and interlined by their owners—*Less salt,* or *Okay but dull,* or *Good with guacamole*—are usually more dependable than those that haven't.

But underlining isn't recommended in general books that other people are apt to read, for it can throw them off their stride. (As the Bible so often does, with its curious italics: "And *there was* a man in Maon, whose possessions *were* in Carmel; and the man *was* very great. . . .") I never have understood why they do that, but I'm sure it would be better reading if they didn't.

811:30
K

BOOKS, Writing of

(See Chapter 13)

CHAPTER THIRTEEN

How Mrs. Arthur Murdock Made Big Money at Home in Her Spare Time, Writing Things

IT WAS AT 3:37 ON A COLD MORNING THAT Mrs. Arthur Murdock's husband's snores crescendoed to a glorious honk, and she said, "Quit snoring, Arthur," got the elbow in the ribs as he rolled over with a WHAAAWWN-GGGHHH and went back to sleep, but she didn't, and Mrs. Arthur Murdock decided that on the following morning she would arise and write. It was something she had always wanted to do.

So she lay awake for a while, planning. Then she drifted off for fifteen minutes' refreshing slumber before the alarm shattered the warm quiet at 6:00 A.M.

At 7:58 the family was off to school and the office, the beds were made, the card table was set up.

Her story would be about a little sick boy. At least, it would start out that way. She knew that.

And then she wrote:

While he seemed to feel all right, that morning
(*dull; not ominous enough; need ominous note*)
The child wasn't suffering, so far as his mother could tell
(*tell who? why "the child"?*)
Apparently the kid wasn't suffering in the slightest
(*oh, wow*)
Though David didn't seem to be in any pain
(*can't he talk?*)
Though David complained of no pain
(*who'd be stupid enough to?*)
Though he didn't complain of a fever or pain
(*need another stanza*)
Though he was pain-free
(*hemorrhoids cured without the knife*)
He wasn't hurting
(*hurting what?*)

And she began to learn many things, among them the fact that there are many ways to say nearly anything, most of them bad.

And she found that she had to triple-space, because her mind kept cleaning up after itself, and she had to write between lines. And, finding that she was presently adrift in a sea of paper, she began buying it in different colors: pink, blue, yellow, white, so she could distinguish first drafts from second, third, and fourth drafts. Then back to pink, and once again around the track.

She found she needed typing practice, and she quickly discarded "the quick brown fox" in favor of "the job requires extra pluck and zeal from every young wage earner," because it seemed more pertinent.

She learned that an electric typewriter caused less backstrain and typed prettier, and that some electric typewriters operate on batteries, for typing outdoors.

She discovered that she kept running out of self-confidence. So sometimes she would copy on her typewriter the first page of a published story by somebody famous, and would sometimes find it didn't look as impressive typed as printed. So she would make corrections and improvements in the margin, or write in a bold hand, "You can do better than this, Mr. Faulkner," the way her English professor used to do. It would sometimes make her feel better.

She learned that real-life conversation seldom sounded real on paper.

She discovered that she loved adverbs: very, rather, practically, strenuously, terribly . . . and that they weakened what they leaned against, so she had to remove them, without anesthesia. She did, relentlessly, sometimes.

She found she hated commas but couldn't do without them. "At the carnival there will be men flipping the flapjacks and costumed waitresses."

She learned that pace and tension seemed to be involved in everything. And she learned not to light all her damp firecrackers at once. And to save out a cherry bomb, if she could find one.

She found that editors were right more often than she was.

She learned to make notes.

And then she wrote:

Preparing Boeuf en Daube isn't hard
(*compared to what?*)
Boeuf en Daube is a delicious dish
(*done to death; everything delicious now*)

To make a good Boeuf en Daube
(*who wants to make a bad one?*)
Did you ever wish you knew how to make Boeuf en Daube
(*what if they said No?*)
For a quick easy solution to
(*Oh, come ON*)

She read that she must use her Unconscious, put a problem on Simmer before she went to sleep; and she did, and she found that it helped, sometimes.

She also found that her Unconscious needed editing; that it could be a bore, and a repetitive one, like a child with a joke. (Dear, you already told me that. No, dear, I said, I've heard it before. I said, SHUT UP.) And she found that it often sulked. If she didn't remove, with alacrity, whatever it sent up on the dumb-waiter and try to use it, it quit sending things up: sat there buffing its nails.

She learned that when the rest of her life was in high gear, so was the writing part of her mind, but then there wasn't time. And when time stretched limitlessly, to write anything was to pry a Sherman tank out of the mud with a teaspoon.

She found that she couldn't write continuously, and that when she wasn't writing she would never know if she were wasting her time or refilling the well.

She found that often the word or action or incident or thought that started a reel to unwinding in her mind didn't appear in the finished piece, a fact that she learned to regard as a mercy.

She learned, after Herculean pasting efforts, that a previously written thing couldn't be pasted into a current thing, for it nearly always showed, and unpalatably, too, a skin-colored Band-Aid.

She discovered that writing was like algebra (which had

also been hard for her)—working with x and not knowing what x was till she was done, and even then not always.

And then she wrote:

> We walked together up the garden path. It was planted on both sides with cabbages.
>
> (*slow, speed it up*)
>
> We walked together
>
> (*walked how? sauntered, raced, limped? self-conscious. WALKED*)
>
> Planted with cabbages, we walked up
>
> (we *were?*)
>
> We walked together up the garden path, poignant with spring's sharp-sweet urgencies and blossoming fatly with cabbages
>
> (*Look, Ma, I'm writing!*)
>
> We walked together down the garden path.
>
> (*DOWN, that's the ticket, faster than up. Don't need the cabbages anyway. Wait a minute, do too. He's about to make that remark about cabbages. Good remark, can't throw it out*)

She found that she quickly acquired a vested interest in what she had already written, would spend three good hours to salvage a phrase from a page and then throw it out.

Also, she learned that whatever she wrote had its length programed within it, like the life span of a species. Heroic measures to prolong it only resulted in something nature never intended, a nonagenarian fruit fly.

She learned that words create thought as often as thought creates words, which was helpful but not always. Sometimes the thought created by the words was a Judas goat that led the rest to places she didn't care to go.

And she learned that there are many kinds of writers—private and public, great and small, careful and careless, good, middling, bad, and many combinations thereof: great careless writers, small careful writers, good-bad writers. And that there are playwrights but no bookwrights, and authoresses—for thus she was sometimes introduced—but apparently no writresses. Only writers.

And she discovered she was constitutionally unable to believe that all other writers didn't have it easy. For it was obvious that their words were hummingbirds, a bright whir of them over the typewriter, seeking only a landing strip. She alone stared at the white paper.

And so she wrote, for it seemed to her that there was, somewhere, a best way for her to say something (and other best ways for other people to say the same thing, though this was fortunately not her concern), and it continued to elude her, which is why she whimpered sometimes.

SUPPLEMENTARY READING

"I don't work all through the night or anything like that, but I do stick with the work. It takes me about two weeks to write a book."

—MICKEY SPILLANE

"Most writers are in a state of gloom most of the time; they need perpetual reassurance."

—JOHN HALL WHEELOCK

"Sometimes I write sober and revise drunk, sometimes I write drunk and revise sober."

—DYLAN THOMAS

"Look sharply after your thoughts. They come unlooked for, like a new bird seen on your trees, and, if you turn to your usual task, disappear; and you shall never find that perception again; never, I say—but perhaps years, ages, and I know not what events and worlds may lie between you and its return."

—RALPH WALDO EMERSON

"You cannot imagine the effort it takes to attain even to ugliness."

—THE PERREY BROTHERS, French architects

"What days off? Days on, I write. Days off, I worry about it."

—STAN DELAPLANE

"Sometimes it takes all my resolution and power of self-control to refrain from butting my head against the wall."

—JOSEPH CONRAD

"Cutting is about the greatest pleasure. That's when you can make happen things you failed to do before. I'm pleased with everything, then I put it together and I say 'Blechh, it's so boring.' I think, 'Why didn't I do that, why did I do that?' "

—MIKE NICHOLS

"It's bad enough to have to write these books without talking about them too."

—SAMUEL BECKETT

"I grant you it's easy enough to choose between a *but* and an *and*. It's a bit more difficult to decide between *and* and *then*. But definitely the hardest thing may be to know whether one should put in an *and* or leave it out."

—Mr. Grand in ALBERT CAMUS's *The Plague*

"Don't."

—Response by J. P. MULLER at an author-editor symposium to the question "Have you any brief advice for would-be writers?"

PART FOUR

I Don't Know about You

"Marriage has teeth, and him bite very hot."
—Jamaican proverb

CHAPTER FOURTEEN

Notes for Lecture Nobody Ever Asked Me to Make

ROCKS IN THE BRIDAL PATH

START WITH JOKE? THAT GOOD HUSB. & WIFE joke, Marr. Clinic. Don't want to though. Something wrong about a woman on hind legs telling jokes. Good joke though. Too bad.

Start with marriage.

All kinds, most not too sacred, just a few. Many not too civil either. Wide range, from How wonderful to How stand it. Some static, some lively, some comfortable like old foundation garment, hold everything together but not much uplift.

Each marriage resembles nation. Own history, language,

customs, laws, military regulations. When civil war dwarfs outside conflict, trouble. (Too pompous. Improve or delete. Who think are?) True though. Happier couples backbite other couples, call it analyzing, don't backbite each other.

Every person expert on marr. whether married frequently, never, or only once. Esp. only once. (Quote Chinese proverb? "See 1,000 pictures once, seen nothing, one picture 1,000 times, seen something." Depends on picture though. Couldn't stand seeing some husbands 1,000 times, some wives either. Depends.)

PROBLEMS:

Wrongthink. American dream, ditto big American promotion, everyone can have happy marriage. Nonsense. Like bathing-suit company, idiot advertising, every woman can have beaut. figure. Can't. Bare-thighed lie. Look around.

Happy people sometimes produce happy marr. not reverse. Some people more talented at marriage, some less. Some resemble ceramics student, tries harder and harder, ash trays get lumpier & lumpier.

Too much talk about marr. Makes people critical of own. More crit. of own marr. than their hi-fi, complexion, social standing, whatever. Put too big load on marriage, blows fuses. Keep shorting out.

Silly. Take marr. like weather. Fact of life, dress for it. Some people don't want bang-up marriage, too much upkeep. Just think they do.

Big misconception: all people should marry. World needs more spinsters, bachelors. Pill can help here. Prob. will. Then urge to couple won't be confused with liking & loving.

Who marry who? More important, *when.* Most people marry too young, babies too soon when should be having fun. Many marr. founder in diaper pail. "Being young with the children"—what mean? Kids think all parents ancient anyway. Want to play with other kids. Parents parents, kids kids.

Would say should marry when personality or character anyway two thirds jelled, like aspic at add-fruit stage. Know what want, not need. Need is terrible basis for marr. Someone says can't live without you, run other way fast.

Opposites attract each other, also attract trouble. Sometimes okay, water each other down. But sometimes infuriating. Merry marries Solemn, likes to make Solemn laugh. Solemn eventually prides self on not laughing.

Opp. in some things good . . . *i.e.*, one likes to drive, one likes to ride. One likes to read aloud, other listen. Other combos pure misery, like hermit-type married to brother-sister-look-alike-pajama type. Hermit-type feels chained to tandem bicycle, wants to get off, beat it into the woods, togetherness-type wants to cry all the time. (Quote Chekhov? "I promise to be a splendid husband, but give me a wife who, like the moon, will not appear in my sky every day.")

Need separate worlds, invite other person in for tea. (Quote Confucius? "In bed, man and wife, out of bed, guests." Sound fellow, Confucius.)

Likes attract too. Placid calls to placid, talk about what they ate yesterday, what eat tonight. Lively calls to lively, What's playing at Rialto?

Some mutual tastes important but people differ, what matters most. No rules. Would say similar feelings about other people, sex, humor, money, fastidiousness, but each to own recipe. In any case shld be able to talk some. Conversation between two consenting adults pleasant thing.

Also: Choose spouse for faults as well as virtues. (Expand if audience not too restive.) Faults contagious, virtues not. Pick faults don't mind catching.

Silliest marr. cliché fault is twisted toothpaste tube; anyone knows it's Kleenex from shirt pocket shredding in washing machine.

Important to remember: Every fault displaces another fault, as olive the gin. Penny pincher at least won't blow it on horses; will have some stashed away if you can get at it. Slob won't dust mantel with white-gloved forefinger.

Always give self strong positive appraisal at all times too. If dull dependable type, tell self at least not flibbertigibbet. If flibbertigibbet, at least not dull dependable type. And so on. Improves morale.

Idiot advice in newsp. marr. columns. If time, quote crazy Italian lady. Angela Petri says woman who starts acting like wife deserves to be ex-wife. Says one way to avoid acting like wife is to act like mistress. Says she and husb. never have trouble finding room at crwded resort because "I simply put on a short bridal veil before walking up to the registration desk. . . . It is important for wives always to be ready to do the unconventional exciting thing." Whee. Wonder if still married.

Importance of not talking things over. Hardly ever improves things. Usually degenerates into dredging things up. Good question to ask self in reprimanding spouse: What trying to do? Unload excess acid? Or improve situation?

Important: In any marriage, some words better not said but probably will be. Then marr. can fall apart like mail-order toaster. Or be epoxied together again so it's stronger than before. Some say. Though maybe because careful thereafter not set it down too hard. Consider.

Possible marr. solution? One-year limitation clause, every marriage. Track records up for review each NYear's Eve, each party sign annually to keep thing going. Interesting

NYear's Eves anyway, better than paper hats. Maybe better marriages too?

DIVORCE. Introd. with L. A. G. Strong's verse?

> *Have I a wife? Bedam I have!*
> *But we was badly mated;*
> *I hit her a great clout one night,*
> *And now we're separated.*
> *And mornin's, going to me work,*
> *I meets her on the quay:*
> *"Good mornin' to ye, ma'am!" says I,*
> *"To hell with ye," says she.*

Lots more div. now. Still everybody claims to be more in favor of marr. than div. Therefore div. not given equal platform time. Maybe doesn't need it. Like second Martini, count on people to think of it anyway.

Question: Which better, two poor marriages or one poor marriage? Prob. two. Two honeymoons that way. Honeymoons usually fun, anyhow.

Difficult subject: divorce vs. children. (Whole other lecture?) Think rotten screaming marriage, nasty icy marriage worse on children than one-parent arrangement. Poor choice. Still many div. children happy little clams. Also, must consider grownups too. Greatest good for greatest number?

Divorce not all bad but expensive. Many women wd get div. if only could afford it. Old Fr. saying, *Money makes la mère go*. Makes le père go too, lots of times. Something to think about all right. Small div. costs much as big wedding, often more.

Divorce should be solitary maneuver. Like dying, or being born. Figure out for self, remember it better. Make sure anything whatsoever is improvement on what you've got. (Quote Monica Baldwin? Check wristwatch. "Leaps over walls—especially when taken late in life—can be extremely perilous. To leap successfully, you need a sense of humour, the spirit of adventure, and an unshakable conviction that what you are leaping over is an obstacle upon which you would otherwise fall down.")

Don't ask friends. Friends will keep long noses out of it anyway if have any decency or cowardice. Otherwise will be blamed, else have you on laps afterward.

Many people who think they want a div. see a marr. counselor. Like going to poodle store to buy cat. Marr. counselor will try talk them out of it, like friendly Suicide Lady at metropolitan Suicide Center. Sometimes good thing. Sometimes just makes div. take longer, cost more.

Usual marriage vows futile. How promise love someone who becomes all unlovable, honor someone who becomes all unhonorable? Maybe promise love constantly as can and be good-natured around the house? Very important. Think about.

Or maybe best, vow to stay worth loving? After all, can only speak for self.

Or maybe not vow at all? (Better sometimes not announce intention. Like dieting, don't announce it, do it.)

I thank you very much.

BEFORE-BREAKFAST BALLAD

Mr. Haskins starts at dawn
To drum his nimble digits on
The banisters, the canisters, and everything in sight.
With all his fingers and a thumb
He drums his little rum-ti-tum
From early in the morning to the middle of the night.

He drums it at the table and he drums it in his bed,
And Mrs. Haskins plans, some day, to shoot him through the head.

For each man riles the one he loves;
Let this be known by many.
Some do it with a moldy joke,
And some with a miser's penny;
(*And drumming, Mrs. Haskins says,*
Is quite as good as any.)

Mr. Bates is quite a hand
At fiddling with his cowlick, and
He twiddles it from sunup till the stars are thick about.
He twists it and he twirls it
And he pulls it out and curls it;
The attrition is terrific, yet he never wears it out.
Mrs. Bates declares the thing is purely automatic,
And aims to wash his hair some day with acid (muriatic).

For each man riles the one he loves;
Let this be known by each.
Some do it with the way they sit;
Some with a trick of speech;
(*And twisting hair, says Mrs. Bates,*
Is quite a little peach.)

Mr. Hyde is really very
Erudite, a literary
Man who knows his Dickens as a shepherd knows his sheep.
He quotes from Copperfield at meals;
His tiniest remark reveals
A solid grasp of Pickwick; Brass and Weller haunt his sleep;
And when he wakes, he'll muse aloud on Nickleby or Fogg.
Mrs. Hyde intends, some day, to feed him to the dog.

For each man riles the one he loves;
The fact is old as pride.
Yet ne'er was there a coin that didn't
Have an obverse side.

(For further information here,
See Haskins, Bates, and Hyde.)

SUPPLEMENTARY READING

"When the satisfaction or security of another person becomes as significant to one as is one's own, then a state of love exists."

—HARRY STACK SULLIVAN

"Civilization, after all, is an act of will."

—STEWART L. UDALL

"The first duty of love is to listen."

—PAUL TILLICH

CHAPTER FIFTEEN

*

Growing Older, or Up: You Can't Have Your Hands Lifted

MUCH IS WRITTEN ABOUT MIDDLE AGE, THESE days, the consensus being that it's an absolutely great time of life, probably the greatest, which you want to postpone as long as you can.

The logic here is like that of the old-time preacher who paints a gorgeous picture of the hereafter while doing his level best to stay this side of it. Indeed, the situations are similar, for Middle Age is certainly closer to the hereafter than Youth is, if youth will stay off its motorcycles and out of the Army, the first of which is unfortunately easier to do than the second.

Perhaps one reason Middle Age is closing ranks and becoming more vocal about itself is because Youth today seems to have the big megaphone.

Advertising agencies and television, primary purveyors of life-styles to the nation, are mainly manned by the young for the even younger, who are naturally more concerned about shiny hair, sweet breaths, whiter white diapers, cavity-free tots, and pimples. These last, if you ever noticed, they don't refer to as "those horrid Youth Spots," although, contrariwise, one hears a lot about "those horrid Age Spots." And by that, they don't mean those retirement homes with the dance directors and organized Bingo; they mean those little brown happenings on the backs of people's hands. Whether the pink spots or the brown spots are the more appealing depends, I suppose, on where you sit.

I would like to report, myself, on Middle Age, which I find interesting and likable country. But I want to make it clear that this is a personal report, and undoubtedly prejudiced. Nearly everyone is more talented at being certain ages than others, some people being natural-born teenagers, for instance (though fewer and fewer are now, I believe, as the teen-age cult grows progressively arcane), and some people being natural-born Old Folks, and so on.[1]

Another thing: most of us arrive at Middle Age by different routes. And we go as we're gaited, at a personal pace that's programed into our genes, though it's complicated by the fact that we're also kicked along by life and circumstance—kicked either from behind, which is a Good Thing, or in the face, which isn't, or anyway doesn't seem so at the time. Indeed, too many bad frontal assaults on the way to Middle Age—sorrow, sickness, marital complexities, and so forth—can effectively spoil the landscape, to the point that it seems quite woebegone country by the time one arrives.

Moreover, depending on talent or inclination, people peak at different ages, some very early indeed. For them, I imagine, Middle Age could be just a long schuss down the slope.

For instance, most athletes and starlets and Homecoming Queens bloom early. So do most poets and mathematicians, who need, besides genius, a certain ability to live *sur les pointes,* which tends to wear off as a life wears on. But most pharmacists, politicians, lawyers, real-estate salesmen, scholars, and many other types bloom later. It takes longer for the brain to develop than for the bosom or the muscles, which is rather a shame. If it were the other way around, people would know better what to do with both, or either.

In general, I think people prefer the age or ages in which their main talents come in the handiest and show up to their best advantage.

I like Middle Age, myself. By Middle Age I mean, by the way, the years from forty-five to sixty-five, give or take a few on either end. This isn't quite twilight, and certainly not bedtime, but, more aptly, the cocktail hour, or, depending on one's persuasion, high tea. After that, you're not middle-aged any more, you're elderly, or old, or dynamically mature.[2]

However, I've noticed that one must be wary of saying one likes Middle Age, at least around the young. They'll suspect you of being brave about it, or of protesting too much.

There are several reasons for this. For one, the young are apt to assume, and often with good cause, that the middle-aged would like to do all the things the young like to do.

Like the big sixteen-year-old girl who assumed I wasn't living fully because I couldn't do the Freak, and tried to teach me. But all she taught me was that a girl built the way she was should wear a girdle while Freaking. On the other hand, I tried, later, to fill in a few chinks of hers, explaining why I thought Robert Frost repeated the last line of his "Stopping by Woods on a Snowy Evening." But I'm afraid all I taught her was how moldy your mind can get if you're not careful. And thus one seems to go along, achieving mainly by-products of his intentions.

Then, another reason that the Young can't honestly see any pluses to Middle Age is that there's a genial conspiracy among people who love their children to make the children feel warmly welcome at all times—feel, indeed, that the parents are psychologically dependent on their presence. This is bolstered by all the published material concerning the loneliness of the parent, once the child has fled the nest, and the bleakness of the bereft mother, painfully groping through the menopausal murk, and so forth. Even a bright child can't be blamed for thinking his presence casts an inimitable glow over the homestead, a sun lamp in which his parents can bask, and for feeling a mite guilty when he turns it off by leaving.

This was probably truer a few generations ago than it is today. Then, people grew older faster, nor were there so many places to go, things to do, or money to do them with.

But now, many quite devoted parents (if they're still speaking to each other, and astonishing numbers are, no matter what you read) feel a near euphoria when the last child is out. As a child progresses from freedom to freedom —from the playpen to the room, from the room to the house to the yard to the neighbor's and to school, and so on, so does a parent progress from freedom to freedom. And when a grown-up child comes limping back, sometimes with one of his own in tow, most parents feel some wholly nonparental emotions, although they usually scratch like a cat in a sandbox to cover them up. Accordingly, it is a rare child who sees that a parent's freedom can be interesting in the slightest, or who is aware that he has derailed anything at all.

Then, finally, the young can't usually understand the middle-aged because they've never been middle-aged. That's where we have the drop on them.

Perhaps the best way to sort out the whole untidy subject is simply to separate the advantages of Middle Age from its disadvantages.

This isn't hard. There is only one disadvantage I can see, and I don't mean poor health, which isn't a general disadvantage; for people usually feel about as good as they ever did, just not quite so bouncy.

(Middle Age is when your chickens come home to roost, all right—all your past sins and indiscretions. But surely there were some good little chickens, too; surely one committed some discretions right along with the indiscretions. Surely the orange juice registers, right along with the gin.)

Indeed, many middle-aged people feel better than ever, because they don't let themselves in for so many hang-overs, overnight camping trips, evenings at the opera and other miserable things. Too, people often outgrow what used to bother them; backaches, headaches, menstrual pains, and so forth. If something serious comes along, it is apt to be later; and even if it comes along right now, most people would rather have it that way than in their teens or twenties or thirties, because they're better able to afford it now, financially and emotionally, too.

No, this disadvantage I mentioned has nothing to do with how you feel, though I admit it's a stunner; and perhaps we'd better get it out of the way first, before we look at all the pluses.

I mean the way one starts to look. Despite one's best efforts, there you go, getting tattier and tattier, things slipping subtly, every which way, or wrinkling for no reason at all, even things you never use.[3]

This can come as a shock to the system, absolutely exploding, as it does, the universal Peter Pan syndrome, which reads, "Everyone else is supposed to grow older and eventually old, except me."

I suppose the discovery that it is actually happening, or that it's happened, takes people in different ways. I remember thinking, at first, It's nothing serious, just a touch of the blight. Of course it'll go away. But of course it didn't.

Then, when I began to suspect things were really getting out of hand, I noticed, in myself, a feeling of embarrassment. Or, more accurately, rather a guilty feeling, as though I had been doing something naughty. Which I might have been, I don't remember, but whatever it was couldn't have been responsible for all this.

A friend of mine first noticed her personal involvement with Middle Age when she was wearing a bathing suit. Her knees, she discovered, had developed double chins. Then, other people find things which were presumably there all along but which become more apparent as distractions grow fewer. A neighbor of mine found, at the age of forty-eight, that one eye was smaller than the other. Presumably it had always been that way, but was more noticeable now, without his former nice stand of hair.

A thing most people agree on, though, is the wisdom of not looking at one's reflection in the side of a chromium toaster, or first thing in the morning, anywhere.

Not that the time of discovery is wholly introspective. Far from it! Right along with one's clinical self-interest come's a cordial interest in one's friends. Lucile is doing okay with the chin line, by the light of a damp match, but what she keeps referring to as "my little bridge" is her little partial plate, right, girls? And Rosemary's keeping the old weight down—understand she eats once a month—but those wrinkles of hers you could plant radishes in, h'm? And take a look at Hermione—smiles a lot, doesn't she? But you better not hand her any corn on the cob or a caramel apple. . . .

Actually, it's quite interesting how people differ in what fetches loose first; for some people were behind the door when the good teeth were handed out, or the lean fat-resistant frames, or the good skins, or maybe even all three.

Now, teeth aren't quite the problem they used to be. Indeed, some teeth enjoy quite a startling renascence in the middle years, if their owners can afford to have them capped, which is called putting your money where your mouth is. After a certain point, they don't look quite real, because teeth ordinarily change color, moving into the gray-green-and-yellow spectrum, while becoming simultaneously more translucent as the years go by. Still, transparent Technicolor teeth are no great shakes either, and the capped ones probably look better than they would have, left alone.

The fat-prone frame is a bigger nuisance, because it demands such continuous battle. Even normally, certain changes take place—what Kingsley Amis called "the lateral fusion of waist and hips," which makes suspenders or braces such a welcome notion for keeping a man's pants up, and makes a straight beltless shift such a pleasure for a woman. And with some people whose enthusiastic metabolisms allow them to gain weight with remarkable ease, one wonders why they keep fighting it, if they do; for it is certainly true that too strict a regimen is a dull disease in itself.

Then there is, of course, the skin—an eventual problem with almost everyone, whether or not it starts out that way. As Dick Hobson put it, after interviewing Hollywood's top plastic surgeon, "Neck-wrinkling and deepening of the 'nasolabial folds' (from nose to mouth) start in the 30's. By the 40's anything goes: frown lines, forehead 'car tracks,' bags under the eyes, 'prune' wrinkles, wattles, pouches breaking up the chin line, cheeks hanging down like dewlaps, sagging mouth, drooping corners at the mouth, jowl formation, double chins, neck stringiness, 'turkey-gobbler neck,' ear lobes that elongate. It's all a matter of the 'oversize skin' of the aging process. . . ."

So all the talk about the special good looks peculiar to Middle Age seems mainly bullfeathers, though peculiar is certainly the word. And it is no wonder that one can get a little frantic, with so many of these things going on at once. It is rather like watching your house go down the hill in a mud slide, trying doggedly, and a little hysterically, to shore it up.

Then, one day, comes the moment of truth; and it comes, actually, as a welcome rainbow, that day when it becomes apparent that it's much more sensible to fix yourself up a snug little cabin off to one side somewhere, and watch the thing go.

It is true that some people can't do this, for professional reasons. Perhaps their livelihoods depend on their looking lively. Or else they have strong personal reasons, like being married to someone a great deal younger, or wanting to be.

Certainly, in these cases, facial injections or plastic surgery—while expensive—can help. Whether it's tiny facial tucks or big box pleats, or a complete rhytidoplasty-blepharoplasty operation that takes off twenty years temporarily, sweeping improvements can be made.

But for people who don't have these compelling reasons, it seems rather futile, because there remains the final embarrassing reckoning ahead. More important, there are always the hands. The hands are the giveaway. To me—I said this was a personal report—there is something wildly out-of-drawing, even obscurely frightening, about the old hands powdering the young nose.

By the way, I believe that one reason so many people today itch to shed a few years is that they often see their acknowledged peers, or elders, on television, looking younger than they do. Not stars, I mean, who have had the benefits of the plastic surgeon's best efforts, but plain people.

I have been doing some television commercials recently, starting a few years ago, at about the same time I was beginning to understand clearly why Queen Elizabeth invented the ruff.

I always find it a heartening experience. The make-up man and the hairdresser relieve me of a dozen years after a couple of hours' hard work, and then they stick close, barely off camera, to see that none sneaks back. Moreover, Harry May, the gallant cameraman, knows every line of my face now better than he knows the road home, and he takes each one as a personal challenge. Harry is very particular about lights. Moreover, it's not my hands, but a hand model's, that stir the product.

While it depresses me a bit to finish a series and turn back into a pumpkin, still I enjoy knowing that most people look considerably better on the gently rounded screen than they do in person.

Then, two other nonsolutions to the middle-aged look should be mentioned, however briefly, before we go on to cheerier and positive things.

One is the increasingly popular Fat Farms, or beauty spas, where one pays astronomical sums to be overexercised and underfed, massaged, herbal-bathed, sauna-ed, and curried. A magazine sent me to one of them, a few years ago, to take the treatment and write a report.

I did so with immense curiosity, expecting heaven knows what (but surely some phoenix would rise, some Venus on the half shell appear out of that rich, steamy amalgam).

It was a luxurious place, misted o'er with tender loving care. That week's twenty-four guests included a couple of pretty co-eds, some comely young wives, and some matrons who looked as though their principal exercise lately had been jumping to erroneous conclusions about how to look younger.

By the time we left, the young women still looked slim and pretty, though hungry, while the rest of us looked like middle-aged women cunningly designed to look middle-aged. There was no real difference between the Before and the After, though we had all had a pleasant time.

It was puzzling, but no more so than clothes and general grooming are. Surely things were simpler, back when grandma wore grandma-clothes and mothers wore mother-clothes and girls wore girl-clothes, and no bones about it except in the corsets of the mothers and the grandmothers.

I wouldn't want to go back to that day, for clothes are more interesting and comfortable now, as well as brighter and easier to take care of. I wish only that the fashion people would quit pushing the notion that young clothes make people look younger, when, so often, they make them look older. There's nothing young about a saucy flash of old knobby knee.✱

Five years, apparently, is about as much as you can chisel, an expert tells me, by careful choice, grooming, and

✱ The ever-shorter skirts, hard enough on the middle-aged, must give the really old people quite a turn. Really old people shrink up anyway, and if your dress looks longer every time you put it on, I should think it would give you the alarming feeling that you're shrinking even faster than you are.

attention to make-up. Speaking of which, the middle-aged woman who adopts the no-lipstick-and-mainly-eyes look—current as I write—doesn't look younger thereby, only aware of what the young are wearing, though it ups her tempo a bit, if that's what she wants. Whereas, when a middle-aged woman wears blue-red lipstick and vivid nail polish, you suspect she's been curled up all day with her collected Dorothy Parker and her Guy Lombardo records, as maybe she was, and, actually, she could have done worse.

As for the Principle of Distraction, so often advocated for the marquisette-sleeve set, I doubt that it accomplishes much. "Distract the eye! Pin a mad brooch to your belt!" scream the barely pubescent copy writers. But I once knew a lady who carried her pet marmoset everywhere for just that purpose, and people would ask, "Who's the old girl with the monkey?"

So let us leave these matters to their own devices, remembering always that wrinkles are not wrinkles but character lines—ask anyone in Hollywood—or, more aptly, lines on a well-used map that's no less interesting on account of them. And if you're packing a few extra pounds, you need something to fall back on, don't you? Don't let your resistance get down, keep some meat on those bones. Ask Grandma.

Or ask Charles McCabe, a gentleman and scholar, who has given the matter considerable thought and deposed as follows:

A face, in a man and in women of a certain age, should be a sort of table of contents to the life of the person who wears it. Interesting people almost always have interesting faces. The more you think about a man's face, the more content he is likely to have for good or evil.

In women, there is a kind of rare beauty in those who have

made peace with their faces, have accepted them, wear them with pride and dignity. More faces have been ruined by plastic surgery, especially in the middleaged, than enhanced by it. To have your character rubbed out of your face is not necessarily to enhance it.

I first read those lines only recently, as I was thinking earnestly about these things; and it occurred to me, with some surprise, that that is, actually, the way I, too, regard the people I know. And so (I wondered then) why not credit them with the same gentle courtesy in regard to me? That seemed only fair. It took me a while. But eventually, Peter Pan flew off with Tinkerbell, which was really a delightful relief, all around.

So let us go on now, to the plentiful pluses.

Now, a great thing about Middle Age is that one is usually in charge of his own life more completely than ever before. This includes both little and big things, both equally satisfying.

Or so I find it. The glorious perquisites of being grown up have it all over the dubious joys of childhood, which have had more publicity than they deserve. Anything that gets so much propaganda is suspect anyway, and in my own case, I remember, the propaganda itself bothered me. Childhood was supposed to be one long frolic on the lea, and though I didn't want to frolic on the lea, wherever and whatever it was, or even know how to, I was glumly aware I should be out there doing it.

I don't think most children today find it very jolly either. A big reason for the fevered teen-age rush for the altar may be the fervent hope that it will stop their being teenagers, which it doesn't always, but you can hardly blame them for trying.

The other day I watched a local junior high pour off

the school bus, half of them looking like Halloween, the poncho-and-dandruff set hard on the heels of the bangs-and-beads. The long hair covered some of the acne but it greased the sweaters, while the tin grins gleamed, and the mini-skirts revealed, in many cases, the maxi-thighs. All bangled, hairy, doggedly in uniform, there was something terribly valiant about them.

I never felt the young-married era was all it is cracked up to be either. Too much hard work, not enough money, too much association with little tiny children—if not one's own, other people's. But now, taking care of little tiny children is more apt to be an elective than a required, which is a big point, right there.

In fact, many people find that for the first time in their lives they're neither Acting Parents nor Acted-upon Children (and it's sometimes hard to decide which is duller, having someone tell you to blow your nose, or having to tell someone to blow his). It is invigorating to be simply an autonomous person, setting your own alarm clock, table, goals, standards, patterns. . . .

Then, equally pleasant—or so I've found it—is having some of the knowledge that can only be bought with years. For one thing, knowledge of moods.

Familiar with my own, now, I can usually spot them coming around the bend, and measure them too, with a *Come on, you know you can't feel this splendid for long* or an *Oh yes, this is the one where I want to bang my head on the floor; it'll pass.* For now they're like relatives I'm better able to put up with, knowing they will eventually go back where they came from. Accordingly I can react less strenuously to other people's moods, too.

Younger people usually can't do this so well: temporary

looks permanent. They haven't learned that curious yeasts are always working on subterranean levels, and so are friends, family, acquaintances, total strangers, and the weather, to add new spices to the soup.

And that so many problems aren't worth worrying about because they'll shortly be replaced by others, often more interesting.

And that many a problem isn't a problem anyway, it's a fact. (The lady across the street from me has problem hair, she says. It is curly. I have problem hair, too. It is straight.)

Then, a corollary to all this is learning with what largess a small effort pays off: the first deep breath, the first brushful of paint, or the note of apology, or the small definitive action of whatever kind—whatever step it is that one wants to take (to use Phyllis McGinley's good phrase) on the thorny difficult road to self-respect. I think many of today's affluent dropouts haven't given themselves time to garner any small victories at all, which is one reason they are flirting today with large defeats.

Another middle-aged advantage is that it's generally possible to throw out some excess mental baggage, if you put your mind on it for a moment. I find I can forget about most of the horrendous things people did to me, back in those tender times when I was walking barefoot over coral, and give at least a rueful thought—no need to wallow—to the ones I probably did to somebody else.

Jo Coudert writes of a brutal incident that discolored years of her life till she decided she could no longer afford the emotional drain. By looking at it hard and clearly, she became able to set it firmly outside her operating realm and shut the door. "Even now," she wrote later, "I cannot write about the memory without a feeling of despair, so remembering does not end the emotion, but its influence on my life is over."

These are practical things, all right. And there are others.

I know now that anything important usually takes six times longer than I expect it to, while the trivial takes virtually no time if I'll just get with it.

And that if I must do an unpleasant chore for someone, I'd better do it good-naturedly or not at all, for otherwise I'll still have the work but none of the credit.

And that Chesterton was right when he said that an adventure is an inconvenience, rightly considered. Appreciating the fact cuts down both outrage and ulcers.

And that Negative Thinking is a great thing, and I don't know why it doesn't get more favorable attention. I've found that the bleak sour knowledge that I can't do something starts enough adrenalin to flowing (or whichever mysterious juice it is) that I can do it, in some fashion or other. Like being chased by a bear, you can jump ten feet, though you otherwise couldn't.

The other side of this, by the way, is equally refreshing. With Middle Age, you can start being honest about what you don't want to do and undoubtedly won't do. Here you can lay a nice base for some comfortable crotchets later on. Indeed, facing these things can become so enjoyable that you're apt to boast a little. (It's a funny thing about me.)

I know, now, that I'll never read *Remembrance of Things Past*, and I know I'll never have the patience to pound the whole half-cupful of flour into the Swiss Steak, and I don't really care.

I know I'll never understand the capital-gains tax, and I don't care about that either.

I'm pretty sure I'll never get proposed to in a gondola (as well as a lot of other places), but that's all right with me. I know I'll never fly a helicopter or speak French like a native of anywhere but Missouri. Or ever achieve that splendid, perfectly-put-together look, because I'll always have a handbag or something else in some evasive color I got because it would go with everything and as a result doesn't go with anything.

And certain matters will remain confused in my mind. Is the British stone twelve pounds or fourteen pounds? (Anyway, aren't they switching to metrics?) Are there two pecks in a bushel? Does "Feed a cold, starve a fever" mean it's bad to make a pig of yourself when you have a cold, because you'll then develop a fever you'll have to cure by starving? Or does it mean that this is the preferred therapy? Though it has been explained to me seven times, it still slides off my mind.

And even words in my own business. *Oxymoron*. I should know what that means. And I just looked it up again this morning. Oh, well . . .

Admittedly, middle-aged memory—now we've come to it—is nothing to brag about. For one thing, it can play you false. I tend more often now to say things like "They don't make —— the way they used to." But whatever word goes into the blank—houses, cough drops, roads, underwear, overshoes, washing machines, face powder, maternity clothes, plumbing, comic strips, cars, soap, baby clothes, hair dye, phonograph records—I usually have to add, on further reflection, Thank God.

Then there is the absent-minded facet. But I think this is overemphasized. If it's absent-minded you're looking for, I'll give you an eleven-year-old. As soon as she gets home from school. If she remembers to get on the bus.

I find, as a matter of fact, that the things I forget

most are the things no one wants to know anyway. Like the name of that little dressmaker back in Chicago in 1949. As for memorizing "Ode to a Nightingale" or lists of battle dates, I know I could if I had to pass a test on it tomorrow.

However, a truly glorious thing about Middle Age is knowing that I don't. The sort of tests you get at this point aren't the kind you have to study for, and that's fine with me. It's a lovely thing to know you can choose your own books or none, or your own alley, job, path, playground . . . just so you pick one to stay alive with, because there are probably so many good years ahead.

Sometimes people pick an absolutely new one, which is refreshing. Equally good is expanding the scope of one you've had before.

Laurence Olivier recently said that he wasn't concerned about his place in the theater any more, but about the theater, which seemed to me to be a thoroughly grown-up remark.

It is true that Sir Laurence doesn't need to worry about his place in the theater, because it is secure, or at least as secure as anything can be in this uncertain world. But neither does the old extra who never made it at all have to worry about his place in the theater, because it is non-existent. Both are free to turn their main attention to something larger and more interesting than themselves, the only alternative being a rather horrid old age.

Thus, in Middle Age, you have the interesting project of evolving—if you haven't already—a self that can be lived with, with reasonable enjoyment; for one is apt to be stuck with it, sooner or later. And another good thing is that one can usually find a little time to do it in, as contrasted with being young, which is so time consuming, as is riding herd on the young, or wishing one knew how to.

Of course, miserable things can happen, later along. The

wrong artery can harden or a fuse can blow, in spite of anything one can do, turning a person into someone he wouldn't ordinarily be caught dead with, though that is what's likely to happen. Still, it is a great plus, the enjoyable times he had with his former self before it took a holiday.

However, this matter of what people do, especially what women do, belongs properly in the next chapter, and I think this chapter is probably long enough now.

NOTES

1. And natural-born parents, too, or natural-born parents of one age child but not another, some being marvelous with babes-in-arms but not so good when the babes climb down, some good with toddlers but not with teens, and some not much good till the child becomes an adult, too, but even that is much better than nothing. Now I've put this down, it doesn't seem to have much to do with what we were talking about, but still I think it's important enough to leave in.

2. At the world's fair in Montreal, they established a place where old people could go to get "day-to-day advice on those pavilions with difficult access," "information on how to tour the Fair without over-exertion," naming it The Dynamic Maturity Pavilion. In a syndicated column I was writing at the time, I said that this seemed on a par with mortical surgeon for undertaker, or the airlines' motion discomfort, meaning nausea, which indeed it gave me a touch of. This is an Alice in Wonderland world, all right, with people cheerily printing all the bad four-letter words, then going around the mulberry bush to avoid saying a word that isn't bad at all, such as old. Like the little dynamically mature lady who said, "Oh shit, I stepped in the doggy doodoo." She was undoubtedly related to the White Queen.

3. "It is eleven Year since I have seen my Figure in a Glass. The last refflection I saw there was so disagreeable, I resolv'd to spare my selfe such mortifications for the Future."
—LADY MARY WORTLEY MONTAGU, in 1757

QUESTIONS & TOPICS FOR DISCUSSION

1. Why are the young so sure they're telling it like it is when most of them haven't been anywhere or done anything yet?

CHAPTER SIXTEEN

Running for Daylight: The Mystique & the Tricycle

IT WAS SEVERAL YEARS AGO THAT THE PROBlem of the Feminine Mystique came along—certainly one of the luxury problems of our time—with news of the two-cars-automatic-dishwasher-beautiful-home-in-the-suburbs-but-something's-missing syndrome, which gives a woman this—how shall we put it?—this empty feeling. This feeling of being somehow incomplete. This feeling of being like a shut-in . . . left out . . . trapped . . . stifled . . .

Squint just a little and you can see us in our jim-dandy dream homes, shrill with wall-to-wall carping.

Then, only recently, the mystique was tooled up to work for the liberation of all women who have been forced behind the "silken curtain of prejudice and discrimination." An organization called NOW * is going to arrange matters so we can compete on equal terms with males everywhere, in offices, professions, political parties, factories, and so on.

But I have a question. May I please stay behind our pretty silken curtain if I want to? Because I think it's nice back here.

I don't mean it's roses all the way. I'll even agree that the militant ladies have a valid complaint or two—for instance, in many fields, women's salaries. We're still not paid as much as men are for the same work, and sometimes better work, which is enough to curdle your milk. Apparently the Equal Employment Opportunity Committee has been pussyfooting around, in seeing that the existing laws concerning employer discrimination against women are enforced.

I don't know. I'm glad that's not my department. I know that we women are able and usually conscientious, dependable as the sunrise. Most of the time. But I know, too, that we all reserve in some little warm corner of our minds the delightful feminine privilege of changing them. The most dedicated careerist can fall in love and follow her new husband to Chile. And babies can still come along at the most awkward times. And when a whole blooming family gets the flu, it's a rare woman who can wholeheartedly do anything but go home and take care of them. If I were an employer, I'm not quite sure what I would do, though I think I'd know how I'd feel, rather as though the immediate vista were planted with time bombs, some apt to go off at any minute (to the Marriage Bureau or to heaven knows what new horizon).

Still, when I think of our feminine advantages, including not being in the muddiest, bloodiest part of whichever war

* National Organization for Women.

we've got going, I think they outweigh the salary business. Indeed, I think we have it so good that I almost suspect NOW of throwing up a crafty smoke screen so the men won't find out how good.

In San Francisco, it is finally legal for women to hang onto cable cars, as men do, when there isn't room to sit down. I happened to be in town, driving behind one on California Street, when a woman fell off, WHAM, like that, landing on her back on the pavement. She was wearing spike heels, wouldn't you know? There's a moral here somewhere, I'm almost sure.

Now, as I get the picture, there are two main types of female misery, besides the less-pay-for-the-same-work group. There are the miserable younger mothers, or MYM's (as I think of them, for we sociologist types love acronyms) and the miserable older mothers, or MOM's.

The first group is miserable because, professionally speaking, they are grounded before take-off: stuck tending babies. The second group—now the kids are grown—is miserable because they're still stuck or because they're not.

I don't think the mystique set credits us with enough brains. Most women want children, many have them on purpose, and most of us realize that when we have a baby today, there's a good chance we'll have to take care of it (as well as the house and the meals), the help situation being what it is, or isn't.

I don't know how NOW aims to solve this one, unless we're to go back to the good old unliberated days when some of us were more equal than others, and a good cook and general factotum was available for ten or fifteen dollars a week.

The equalization of women via the marvelous new conveniences has equalized us back into doing our own scutwork. Someone has to do things: vegetable bins must be cleaned out, babies diapered and kissed, floors swept; and as the old Galician proverb has it, "If I am a lady and you are a lady, who will bed the sow?"

The NOW people seem to regard this simple fact with a sense of outrage. But I don't see why. And I don't think most women do; for most of us consider having a baby to be more than laying an egg for someone else to hatch. We'd rather have a hand in the hatching, at least into its teens. Sixteen years of child rearing isn't necessarily sixteen years in the desert.

Then, another thing I've noticed: these militant mystique people seem to assume that we've all buried splendid careers under a pile of ironing.

This is a highly dubious assumption. Women of genius usually have the compulsion to make it work, in spite of anything and everything. This seems to be part of the genius. Look at Madame Curie, Rebecca West, St. Thérèse. . . . As for the rest of us, some discover a distinct professional interest or talent early, some later along, and quite a number not at all (as opposed to NOW's flattering theory that we're all innately chiefs; no Indians).

Now, with those who do find a compelling interest, early or late, it isn't necessarily plain sailing. Though keeping it warm through the nursery-bound years and eventually getting back to it is usually possible, in this lively TV-paperback-radio-night-class-refresher-course age, sometimes husbands try to make it impossible.

The problem can take several forms. Sometimes the little fellow fears, with justification, that his wife will find the work more interesting than she finds him, which can result in naughty tantrums, eventually forcing a woman to decide, one way or the other.

Sometimes the mere thought that his wife can earn money is unsettling to a traditionalist husband who feels strongly that the husband should be the giver of all good gifts. Some men tie this up with sex, in some funny way; feel they have to support the woman they go to bed with. Often they can't help feeling like this, for it's the way they were brought up.

In these cases, a woman can often use her talents satisfactorily in volunteer work, for this sort of husband doesn't mind his wife's carrying slops for free in the local hospital; he just can't stand her carrying a briefcase or a script and getting paid for it. It's a good thing there are so many interesting kinds of volunteer work that need doing, too (and if they didn't get done, some communities would virtually fall apart).

Sometimes a hard choice must be made: the husband vs. the work. Though it can also be an easy choice, as I found it once myself, for there seemed no comparison between the general worth and appeal of the two.

Then, sometimes, a man who is perfectly happy to have his wife pursue work that interests her will be transferred to a place where there isn't the remotest possibility of her doing it. This is too bad, but it isn't the end of the world. There is still a lot of it left if she will look around.

As long as men and women marry, and women have children, women will be broken-field runners, zigzagging down the field, dodging or tackling large obstacles, and running for daylight.

In any case, it is important to remember that most husbands make compromises, too. Most would prefer a freighter trip to the South Seas to orthodontia for three children; yet they usually opt for the teeth.

But back to the remaining group, the women who have no particular bent but still get jobs. Menial jobs, the NOW people call them, angrily. But they're not menial, they're simply necessary, and they outnumber careers, a hundred to one: jobs in offices, canneries, shops, banks, mills, mailing rooms, restaurants. . . . Moreover, jobs are what many of us want.

Women work at jobs like these for many reasons: some because they must; some because they want to do something that's rewarding in some fashion or other but not wholly involving, so they can put it out of their minds the minute they leave; some for a specific reason, like travel or the children's education; some out of pure habit, because life without going out to a job seems only half a life.✱

But often, looming large behind any of these reasons is the fact that it's rather dull at home, and lonesome. A few generations ago, in big houses with live-in relatives and maids of all work and children around more often, a woman had company. But now, most women at home are there alone; and while it may be dull at work, somewhere else, still there's someone to talk to about how dull it is.

Also, it's odd, but the more automated the house is, and the more efficient the girl running it, the less satisfying it can be. (Not always; with true dedicated natural-born housewives, after they've done a week's work in a day, they'll go right ahead and squiggle some butter curls or polish the horse brasses.) But the less devout type will turn on the lawn sprinklers, set the button on the self-cleaning oven, start the dishwasher, do a washing, put the no-iron sheets back on the bed, thaw something for dinner, and end up with a bad case of Domestic Jet Lag, from covering too much country too fast without being truly involved in it. It

✱ And certainly the job world can be a vivid cozy world, full of gossip, intrigue, companionship, mutual effort. It's also a place to wear clothes. It can be pretty frustrating to see all the pretty advertised clothes that you haven't a reason in the world for getting.

is an increasingly frequent female complaint, the chief symptom being a tendency to nag everybody in sight and read the Help Wanted columns of the daily paper. It is also the reason why a woman will make her own currant conserve at $7.50 a pint if she counted her time, or hand hook her own hearthrug from Many Attractive Stamped Patterns Available.

Too, philosophical types can find themselves in a quandary. After cleaning the house (though it really wasn't too bad before, and the idea of even touching it tomorrow is boring to the point of nausea), as well as building an interesting meal (the family would have been as happy with chops and scalloped spuds)—after doing these things, they can find themselves wondering, uneasily, What for?

For it's inconclusive business, this housekeeping, this cooking. The truth seems to be that women face the frightening fact of leisure time sooner than men do, these days. Boredom is a big operative force in our economy.

Actually, a fair percentage of life is boring, and I don't understand the people who say you should never be bored because the world (as they put it) is so full of a number of things, and so on. That's just it, it certainly is, and so many of them are boring.

Certainly, a job isn't the infallible answer; a job can be another bore. Indeed, a job can be many things, including a stopgap, a solution, or a postponement of the good old eyeball-to-eyeball confrontation with one's self, we women being as various as we are.

I've done both—stayed at home all day, feeling like a body of ignorance surrounded by unmade beds, and worked in an office, a bundle of nerves surrounded by unwritten radio scripts. Neither was quite right for me. I thought at the time that for every suburban matron extending the

Kaffee klatsch to put off straightening the hall closet, there is probably a working matron dreaming over the coffee break of the coming weekend when she can get her hall closet nicely sorted out.

Thinking of these things recently, I happened on Robert Ardrey's book *The Territorial Imperative*. One of his findings, after he made a comprehensive study of many kinds of life, seemed so pertinent to the subject of women and what we should be doing about ourselves, if anything, that I want to mention it here.

I refer to his conclusion that creatures require three basic elements: Identity, Stimulation, and Security, the least important being Security.

This seemed to me to square with the observable facts. The most miserable people are long on security and nothing else: convicts, retired old people shunted to dull sidings, and a number of affluent youngsters in desperate search for the other two missing factors. Historically, too, people and countries have been quick to kick Security overboard when things became too dull, to go crusading or fighting or exploring. We seem to need circuses a bit more than bread, as well as a slight feeling of belonging to the circus, too, if only to sweep up the popcorn.

And so it is with women, it seems to me. What problems we have stem from or depend on those three things—three wheels on the tricycle; and I've found the concept of great interest, by the way, in diagnosing myself and my friends. How is *her* tricycle rolling along, I ask myself, without, of course, much hope of an intelligent answer. I can only guess. It's hard enough to make a fair appraisal of my own, which has had some balky times, all right, first one square wheel and then another. Anyone would think I'd put the thing together myself.

However, it seems to me important that we occasionally examine our own personal three wheels and see what makes them go.

Take Security. It can be downgraded too far by people who count on the ravens to provide, or the Welfare Board. But it can be extravagantly upgraded, as well, by people who keep right on chasing it when they already have as much as one can logically expect, this side of a six-foot box. And somebody keeps raising the ante on Security, too, so that it's all mixed up with the superfluous. A woman needs to have her own definition clear in her mind, I think, or she can find herself taking a dull job to earn the second color TV.

It is immensely important that a woman be interested—at least most of the time—in what she is doing.[1] Accordingly, we must all be honest, at least with ourselves, about what really stimulates us. We're all different, and, so often, what is supposed to stimulate us doesn't, and vice versa.

A woman I know tried to become active in the new local Environmental Theater but discovered that it bored the daylights out of her. What stimulates her is rooting geraniums. She takes little bits (I never could figure out which bits to take, myself) and roots them in separate pots and waters them and moves them about and enjoys them—seventy-six at last count—and to her they are aspirin, prayer, a night at the theater, all wrapped up. This is stimulation, too, not just amusement; puts new fire in her eye and spring in her step.

Another friend of mine, who loves to knit, decided, finally, that she had enough sweaters and so did her family and friends. So she began giving knitting lessons to the women at the local penitentiary, and what had been passive amusement for her thus became stimulating. And, of course, it oiled the penitentiary ladies' Stimulation and Identity wheels as well as my friend's, and it was a most satisfactory operation all around.

But sources of stimulation are legion, as are women; what is vital is to know your own.

Then there is the third wheel, Identity, which I sometimes think is the most important wheel to keep in fair running condition (because if it isn't, there's nothing for it but to mess up someone else's).

There are many sources of it. Some, for instance, are nourished mainly by family or tradition ("I'm a Cooperthwaite, of the Winston Cooperthwaites"), which is better than nothing, though it can melt like a popsicle in the sunshine if I move to a place where nobody ever heard of the Winston Cooperthwaites.

And many Identities are fattened when their owners join up with a larger one—a club or country or a church or the Symphony Society. . . .

And many a woman gets into the habit of taking her identity wholly from her husband or her children, to her peril. For they may die on her, or get bored with her (but who doesn't know *that*, since Philip Wylie first trumpeted Momism from the mountaintop).

Creative activity is probably the big source of Identity. ("I'm the one who produced that.") Eric Hoffer spoke truly when he said that "nothing so bolsters our self-confidence and reconciles us with ourselves as the continuous ability to create; to see things grow and develop under our hand, day in, day out."

And it's a lovely thing that there are so many kinds and levels of it. For Creativity doesn't necessarily mean crafts and water colors and pots, though the thriving Art Centers in many places would have one thinking so. Another confusing factor is the current emphasis on the Hideous and the Happening, and the recent art cults from Pop to Poop, which may well have set good old Creativity back twenty years.

The only workable definition of Creativity I know is doing something that's usually difficult, nearly always joyous (at least in part), and engrossing to the point of love, resulting in something that only you could have or would have made in quite that way. I've seen truly creatively done glossaries, soups, businesses, bylaws, fences, sermons, and a hundred other things. This kind of creative work is the most tiring of anything, as well as the most reviving.

The rest is Occupational Therapy (*cross-stitch the x-squares pink*), which is disappointing business if you mistake it for Creative, but certainly has its important place. At the end of this chapter is the best apologia I ever saw for handwork.[2]

In the last analysis, a woman had better run her own tricycle, insofar as she can. I've noticed that people who depend too much on other people—who have to feel needed and keep talking about it—seldom are. (Oh God, here comes Aunt Wilma again.) But if they are necessary to themselves, they are generally necessary to other people, whether they like it or not. Every tub must sit on its own bottom, or as the French put it, more prettily, *Pas de leur en connu.*

So it seems to me that the feminine problem isn't quite so clear-cut as the NOW people would have us think, nor are we women quite so desperate about it either. In our practical and inventive way, with bits of bailing wire and Scotch tape and an emery board, I think we show an astonishing talent at keeping our tricycles on the freeway.

I doubt that anyone ever rollicks through a lifetime, on three perfectly round, easy-rolling wheels. And if it ever seems that way, watch out, for there's probably something or somebody about to poke a stick into the spokes.

Still, no one is the worse for understanding the minimum mechanics of making her own three wheels go around. That way, she can give herself periodic checkups, discover whether she's on two wheels or one, discover what needs fixing, but, one way or another, keep pedaling.

NOTES

1. "Life is not lost by dying! Life is lost
Moment by moment, day by dragging day,
In all the thousand, small, uncaring ways—
The smooth appeasing compromises of time. . . ."
—STEPHEN VINCENT BENÉT

2. "It's an oldfashioned cure for restlessness, my dear, in case you ever need it. Remember that it has been successful for hundreds of women. I'm no fool, am I? Well, I haven't traveled without my tapestry since my girlhood, and you should see the splendid suites of furniture covered by my handiwork, testimonials to worries of all sorts. Whenever I have felt nervous, vaguely dissatisfied, irresolute, or frankly wretched, I have sat by myself. Each embroidery contains hundreds of stitches which are cross-stones of sorrow, the death beds of boredom. In many a gaily flowered seat, my happiness lies buried. People spend time and money being exorcised; psycho-analyzed, they call it, seeking relief for body and soul. I think that a good long mechanical task that requires a minimum of attention, and the soothing action of the hand as it dips over and under the canvas, is the very best means of pinning down our weaknesses and chloroforming them. Stitch the horrors down, my dear, and they shan't return to plague you; they are killed by the stab of the needle. Of course, during peaceful intervals, I have laid my work away for months, but when I need it, there it is, as convenient as a box of aspirins against a cold."
—ANNE GREEN, *16 Rue Corta Bert*

CHAPTER SEVENTEEN

*

When You Buy Brooms

I LIKE TO DYE MY UNDERWEAR AND NIGHT-gowns, periodically, when I get tired of white, which I buy to begin with, on purpose. Such pretty dyes are available now, and they don't stain the sink the way they used to. You don't even have to stir all the time; just once in a while, and the rest of the morning you can stretch out on the sofa and think about things.

The other day, as I lay dyeing, I was remembering where I first got the idea. It was from a lady named Oppum. Mrs. Oppum.

There we were, trying on clothes in one of those communal dressing rooms you find in the *basse couture* establishments; and I was admiring her Kelly-green underwear. She explained to me her dyeing procedure, and we became quite friendly—exchanged names and all that—and I can see her to this day, a plump short woman with little round teeth, like beans. Moreover, I see her every time I fill the dye kettle.

My dye kettle sits, by the way, on the high shelf in the floor-mop-and-ironing-board closet. When I open that closet door, I can't help but see the floor mop—rather a ratty-looking affair, because I don't like to spend good money on things like that. And simultaneously I see the puffy, tidier-than-thou face of an acquaintance, who once caught me mopping with it. She regarded it with disfavor. "I'd lose my *mind,*" she said, and now I give her a mental dirty look whenever I mop. Sometimes people try to run me too much.

The fact is, one's life eventually contains quite a cast of characters, appearing at odd moments, then fading and appearing and fading again, like the Cheshire cat . . . hundreds of them, some with names, some with no names; no matter, they're indelibly there, and it is curious to think that you are similarly materializing moment by moment in other people's awarenesses, too.

Sometimes, I've found, this happens directly: I see or hear such-and-such and I think of So-and-So.

Like kelp. I mentioned earlier, I believe, the lank seaweed strung with shiny brown sacs that pop so satisfyingly underfoot, on the beach where I live. Walking along the sand one day with my friend Erwin, the painter, I found an especially good one for him to step on. But he wouldn't, out of respect, I think, for its recent demise as well as for its basic good looks. I felt abashed and haven't popped any more myself, at least when he was around. And still, whenever I see it . . .

Or it will happen sometimes in a dependable Tinker-to-Evers-to-Chance sequence, both backward and forward.

The lady behind the dry cleaner's counter told me once, apropos of I don't know what, that her grandmother had a standard answer for dull questions like "How are you feeling, Granny?"

"Noody noddy when you buy brooms," Granny would say, meaning six-of-one-half-a-dozen-of-the-other-what's-the-difference-let's-talk-about-something-more-interesting.

I've found this useful indeed. "What are we having for dinner?" "How's the work going?" they ask. Noody, noddy, I reply, and see the dry-cleaner lady and think of her grandmother. Or else, stopping at the dry cleaner's, I see the lady, and think of her grandmother, and bump into Noody noddy . . . either way.

So it seems to me none of us can measure the space we occupy in someone else's mind, or count the times we re-enter it (which certainly gives the lie to the tired remark "You wouldn't worry what people think of you if you knew how seldom they do"). And I suppose none of us ever quite knows what he is remembered *for,* either, any more than we ever know for what precise reasons we are loved, if we are, which* is probably just as well.

I've found that people even materialize in the privacy of the bath, though I'm sure they'd be dismayed to know it. I know a lady—a truly delicate blossom—who became upset and highly vocal about the lack of breeding evidenced in someone's home where she had been a guest. In each bath-

* "You do use a lot of whiches," my editor observed mildly, one day, reading a manuscript of mine. So I often change them to something else now, and think of Julian at every which.

room, she said, the tissue (her word for toilet paper) was hung with the end of the paper curling down over the *front* of the roll, mind you, instead of discreetly down the back.

I had never heard, till then, that it mattered; didn't know there was any toilet-paper protocol. But I've been mighty careful ever since, I can tell you, when I replenish the bathroom supplies, and I think of my fragile friend every time.

Just as—in other rooms and places—I so often think of a girl named Marie, the talented housekeeper who was my next-door neighbor when I was first married. Come summer, her fireplace became a garden instead of a waste-basket, as mine did, and her money never ran out ahead of the month, and her table cigarette lighter worked. I respected her very much.

One day I watched her as she melted down some candle stubs, for some undoubtedly practical purpose. "Everything seems to be good for something," she commented. (It is interesting to ponder, by the way, why a simple statement made by someone else usually seems more valid than something one says one's self. Had I said that, I don't think I would have listened.)

However, I never forgot it, and I think of Marie often, for I've noticed that everything does, indeed, seem to be good for something, even the dust on the dining-room table, which is handy for writing phone numbers on, or reminding you that a little formality isn't necessarily a bad thing, and perhaps you'd better stop eating all the time in the kitchen.

And—now I mention it, because it seems to follow me around—the kitchen. How people-impacted a kitchen can get! My own holds so many distracting association-items that it's no wonder some recipes turn out the way they do.

There is my French whisk ("Shut up, you'll use it all the

time," said Eloise, who gave it to me, and she was right, I do, and I hear her, every time I pick it up).

There is my tin saucepan from the variety store. (A girl named Carol seems to live in it. I forget her last name, but I see clearly her little close-together eyes and fancy clothes. She was along when I bought it, and she said, "You don't want a cheap little pan like that," but I did. It seemed to me then just the pan to boil an egg in, and, indeed, it still does.)

Then, foods, and ingredients, and, of course, recipes. I can't help thinking of Mrs. Murgatroyd whenever I mix Mrs. Murgatroyd's Meatloaf, or of Jane Perry when I bake Jane Perry's Banana Cookies, or of Mary when I smell curry. Nor can I see an English muffin without thinking of my good friend Brandy.

A creative man, Brandy invented a new treatment for the Sunday-morning English muffin: split and butter it, douse it gently with good maple syrup, then toast it under the broiler.

This is chewy, like a torte. In fact, Brandy christened it the Sawfry Torte, because it turneth away wrath (his wife is becoming impatient, lying in bed, wondering what took him so long).

And it has occurred to me that I, too, am perhaps permanently affixed to some recipe or other, in certain people's minds—cemented to Maxie's Franks, say, or Stayabed Stew —not that it bothers me if it turns out all right for them and they don't get mad.

John McNulty tells of the Irish storyteller in County Kerry, who said to him, after telling a story (in his whitewashed-walled cottage with the turf fire burning), "Do you see what I have done? Without passing a solid thing from my hand to yours, I have put words into your head, and they're the words of a story. Now you will carry the story back in your head to America, and perhaps you will tell the story, too, or perhaps you will write it down. And after a while I will die, but over in America will be a story of mine going around, without ever stopping from going, one to another, and so I won't be dead at all, in one way of thinking it. That's what I have done this day. God bless!"

I find it heartening to think about this curiously stubborn aliveness that one has in other minds, from whatever indelible words or pictures you unconsciously planted there, and that they have in yours. Like fireflies in firefly country. Or like stars—stars in a dark summer sky. Random instant after instant, look nearly anywhere, and a light winks on.

So I'll let you go now, as a lady said to me, finally, on the telephone the other day, after I had talked and talked and talked. I thought it was a good way to end almost anything.

APPENDIX

On the twenty-ninth day.

INDEX

(NOTE: I had never done an index before this one, and after I volunteered, I wished I hadn't. Establishing an index presents similar problems, I suppose, to those of establishing a nation, though I never tried that. In each case, laws must be made and obeyed, or chaos prevails. Even so, some chaos creeps in.

My own laws were these: 1. anything or anyone I quoted would be italicized; 2. a clue as to subject matter would be provided, when convenient, and 3. only interesting things would be indexed, the dull ones left alone.

Still, special circumstances kept arising. For instance, inasmuch as two of *Hoffer, Eric*'s quotations appear on the same page of the book, one entry for both might have sufficed. But it seemed to look nicer the other way.

Then, inasmuch as names are always indexed backward, perhaps—I thought—subheads should be backward too: "Desires, insistent" and "Superflous, search for the" or "Saks Fifth Avenue, before going hog-wild at, things to think about." But as it began to sound dumber and dumber, I realized that I'd have to shift out of reverse at some point, else "backward ran the entries till reeled the mind," to quote Wolcott Gibbs, and now I'll have to index him. This sort of thing can lead to very cross indexing, and so I stopped before my disposition got entirely out of hand.)

Index

* St. Bernard I forgot to include in the book.

$4.95

PEG BRACKEN

I DIDN'T COME HERE TO ARGUE

Here are a wondrous variety and startling range of original observations, graced with lyric prose, laced with laughter, alive with anecdotes, and sparkled with surprises. For the millions of readers who delight in Peg Bracken's writing, there's cause for celebration in this bright new book. Those who haven't met her couldn't have a happier introduction.

Feel a little dizzy on the marriage-go-round? "Notes for Lecture Nobody Ever Asked Me to Make" is for you. Is your generation gap showing? Read "Don't Trust Anybody over Fifteen or Talk to Anybody under Forty." Tired of friends who are going to dash off a best seller just as soon as they can spare a little time?